GRAS

the Nettle

Taking action immediately in order to deal with a difficult or unpleasant situation

A step by step guide to tackling poor performance, unacceptable behaviour and poor attendance in the workplace

Anthony Dance

www.graspingthenettle.com

Shield Crest

© Copyright 2014 Anthony Dance

All rights reserved

ISBN 978-1-910176-11-5

MMXIV

Published by
ShieldCrest
Aylesbury, Buckinghamshire, HP22 5RR
England
www.shieldcrest.co.uk

REMEMBER? "YOU DO NOT DO THIS
BUT YOU SHOULD DO"

THANKS FOR GIVING ME THE MOTIVATION
AND INSPIRATION IN WRITING THIS.

ANTHONY

Dedications

My thanks to the many poorly performing employees who have crossed my path: if it had not been for you, I would not have learnt so much, or have been able to help so many.

Anthony Dance

Who should read this book?

- Newly appointed managers
- Experienced managers who need personal development in this area
- Executives or Middle Managers responsible for Line Manager Performance
- HR professionals responsible for employee performance

Introduction

GRASPING the poor performance nettle.

Did you know that it is possible to grasp a stinging nettle without getting stung? All you need to do is grab hold of it boldly, quickly and by using the right technique.
Tackling poor performance or poor behaviour should be approached in the same way. Confront a performance or behaviour issue quickly, confidently, and in the right manner, and it is possible to do this (the most difficult and challenging of all management tasks) without too much pain.

Read and digest the critical information outlined in this manager development book and follow the GRASPING the Nettle steps and you will find that tackling poor performance is not as difficult as you may think. This is a *must read* for all 'people' managers because by using the unique procedures, tips and techniques outlined in this book, you will be able to address performance issues effectively, professionally, fairly and reasonably.
Reading this book before tackling a performance issue will certainly minimise the risk of complaints, grievances and spurious tribunal claims.

The Author

My first manager position was general manager of a small supermarket in London. The branch I took over had a sickness and absenteeism problem: every week people were calling in sick.

On reviewing the absence records, I identified a warehouse operative called Derek who was obviously taking advantage of the company's sick pay benefits. Records clearly showed he had taken many sick days prior to weekends, holidays etc. Never having tackled an issue like this before, I contacted my middle manager for permission to address the issue.

The middle manager was very positive about me 'grasping the nettle' and gave me the go-ahead. Encouraged by my middle manager's comments, I called Derek to the office to talk about his sickness record. I never really got started, because Derek refused to discuss the matter. "You have no right to talk to me about my sick record, it is none of your business," he said. He then proceeded to storm out of the office shouting 'bullying'!!

Taken aback, I contacted my middle manager again to tell him what had happened. Summoning up many years of middle management experience my middle manager said… "Speak to HR," which I duly did. Following confirmation from HR that I <u>did</u> have a right to discuss someone's attendance record, I asked Derek to come to the office again. Again I did not really get started as Derek said "I don't care who you have spoken to, my sickness is my business and nobody else's." Getting more frustrated I contacted the HR department again and explained the situation. I asked the HR manager if he would explain the position to Derek as he was refusing to discuss the matter with me. After a great deal of reluctance the HR manager agreed to talk to Derek, but not before voicing negative comments about my competence.

Following discussions with the HR manager, Derek agreed to talk to me, but only if he had someone else in the office to witness what was said. I naively agreed, and the company union representative joined myself and Derek in the office. Needless to say, the meeting did not go well. There was a shouting match, the union rep accused me of bullying and the meeting concluded with both Derek and the union rep storming out of the office, threatening me with a formal complaint.

Shocked, bruised and feeling stupid, I felt that at least I had got an important message across. Ten minutes following the meeting, I received a call from the HR manager. "We have received a complaint from the union rep regarding your aggressive style; they do not wish to make a formal complaint but felt their concerns should be noted." I was then lectured about the risks of having an aggressive management style.

A short time after speaking to the HR Manager I was contacted by my middle manager who said "Well, you made a right old mess of that then, didn't you!!" He then proceeded to give me a reprimand for not handling the situation correctly.

Obviously this incident did put me off from tackling poor performance for a while, but I did learn from the experience and it did actually make me more confident and determined. Over the years I became skilled in poor performance management which helped me climb the corporate ladder to Executive level.

Never, ever forget the fact that 'employers have rights too' and always remind your poor performers of this.

Final note: Derek left the organisation shortly after our conversation; the union rep took a little longer.

Contents

Poor Performance

Chapter 1
Poor Performance

'When an employee's performance <u>or</u> behaviour falls below the required standard'
(Legal definition)

Chapter 1 – Poor Performance

- Definitions
- Why the problem?
- Whose Responsibility?
- Financial cost of poor performance
- Cost to manager credibility
- Why the reluctance?
- What is the solution?

Definitions

Poor performance

Poor performance can be legally defined as: 'when an employee's performance or behaviour falls below the required standard'.

What is significant about this definition is that it brings both performance <u>and</u> behaviour under one definition. However, poor performance and poor behaviour need to be managed differently.

Poor *performance* is when an employee's performance <u>consistently</u> falls below the required standard as outlined in the job description. The job description is part of the contract of employment, so not doing the job is basically a breach of contract on the part of the employee.

Poor *behaviour* is not as straightforward, as there is a long list of behaviours that would constitute poor behaviour. The rule of thumb I believe is that when an employee's words or behaviours negatively affect business, productivity, team performance, or team motivation, then the employee is behaving poorly. If you do not like an employee's behaviour but <u>it does not</u> affect the above, then this is probably 'personality'. Managers have a right to challenge poor behaviour but they do not have a right to change someone's personality.

Inconsistent performance
Every employee's performance can fluctuate at times but truly inconsistent performance can be defined as: **'When an employee's performance falls below the required standard most of the time'**

Inconsistent

'Irregular, unpredictable and uncertain performance'

Why the problem?

Executives/Business owners influence culture

It is a simple fact that employees perform or behave below the required standard because key people at the top of the organisation are allowing them to do so. Executives/business owners who tolerate poor performance or discourage the tackling of poor performance create a culture where poor performance is accepted rather than the right performance being expected. Executives/business owners do this by:

- Going into panic mode when the word tribunal is mentioned.

- Fault finding in the way the manager handled the situation, focusing on the few things that the manager could have done differently rather than the many things that the manager did right.

- Blaming the manager for the cost and disruption caused when grievance or stress claims occur.

- Not supporting the manager when all the manager is trying to do is improve performance.

- Appease situations, giving employees the benefit of the doubt when judging on grievance accusations.

- Moving poor performers to other places/positions rather than sorting the problem out where it is.

- Paying off employees too quickly with payments that appear to reward poor performance.

These actions and behaviours discourage rather than encourage the addressing of poor performance at manager level, and when that happens, a negative attitude towards the management of poor performance is created.

Culture Influencers

'The values and beliefs of key people that influence attitudes, behaviours and customs within an organisation'

Whose Responsibility?

Manager responsibilities – When you take on the job as manager, supervisor or team leader: whatever the title, you automatically become responsible for the performance and development of the people within the team. Tackling the under-performing employee and correcting poor behaviour when it occurs is part of the job description; it is what managers are paid to do and they have to do it when necessary. Unfortunately, many people take on the manager job without taking this into consideration and get a shock when they are confronted with a poor performance/behaviour issue for the first time.

Management issue not an HR one – Poor performance is clearly a management responsibility, not an HR one. It is not HR's job or responsibility to sort out our poor performers. HR does have a supporting responsibility and they should ensure managers have clear procedures to work with and processes to follow in order to maintain consistency across the organisation.

Company responsibilities

Executives/business owners are indirectly responsible for the performance and behaviour of all employees but do this through their managers. Executives *are* however responsible for ensuring that managers are given the right training and support in order for them to address performance issues correctly. It is a fact that when a manager takes over from a 'good' manager they are likely to inherit few issues, but taking over from a 'not so good' manager they are likely to inherit many.

Too many new managers (new to the manager role) are put into situations where they inherit difficult, complicated, long-term performance issues without any training or support.

Responsibility

'Being in charge of someone and making sure that what they are required to do is done satisfactorily or well'

Financial Costs

Financial Costs

There have been many surveys conducted with the aim of calculating the costs of poor performance in a business. All have ended up with 'guesstimates' because of the difficulty in accurately calculating the loss.

The situation is clearer however when analysing financial statistics of a department function that is operated by a manager who tolerates poor performance rather than addressing it.

Operating costs

Managers who tolerate poor performance normally have unnecessary costs due to staff turnover, high sickness, lower productivity and so forth.

It has been proven that operating costs can be as much as **15%** higher in a department/function that is suffering from performance issues compared to a department that is not.

Loss of business potential

Managers of 'sales based' functions who tolerate poor performance will <u>always</u> lose business opportunities and not maximise the full sales potential within their function. Case studies within the retail industry have proven that the difference to annual sales between a good manager and a not-so-good one can be as much as 25% additional sales over a period of a year.

Tolerating poor performance costs businesses dearly in increased costs, lost sales opportunities and service credibility.

See Cost of Poor Performance: Case Studies in Appendix 1.

Tolerate

'To allow without prohibiting or opposing'

Credibility Costs

Manager respect and credibility
No Manager or Executive would doubt the financial loss to the organisation by tolerating poor performance, but there are other losses that are equally costly, such as:

- Loss of credibility and respect for the Manager in the eyes of 'good' team members.
- Managers also lose credibility with their Bosses which in turn affects their career prospects.
- Managers lose self-esteem, self-motivation and confidence.
- Good employees leave because they do not like 'carrying' poor performers.
- Good team members lower their standards in line with the poor performers.

Mentoring Note
In my time as a Middle Manager, a key part of my role was **succession planning**. Many Line Managers were interested in career progression and it was up to me to identify middle manager potential and develop it. I would not endorse any line manager's application for a middle management role if they could not address poor performance. The main reason for this was because if they could not tackle employee poor performance then they would not be able to tackle line manager poor

performance, which is certainly a great deal more challenging.

This is one of the principal reasons why many line managers fail to progress to middle management roles.

Credibility

'The quality of being believed or trusted'

Why the reluctance?

If the cost is so great then why the reluctance? Poor performance management is complicated: tackling a gross misconduct issue is relatively simple as there are normally definite facts to work on and a clear process to follow. Poor performance however is not so straight-forward, as facts tend to be ambiguous and there are few clear processes to follow. Poor performance management is often:

- **Complicated** – The employee may have been under-performing for a long time and nobody has tackled them about it before. Their performance may be inconsistent: sometimes acceptable, sometimes not – and there may not be any history of poor performance on the employee's personnel record.

- **Time consuming** – Managing a poor performance issue is certainly time-consuming because it involves analysis, planning, meetings and often a great deal of documentation. Finding the time to deal with a performance issue properly is something many managers struggle with.

- **Uncomfortable** – Tackling poor performance is often unpleasant and can take managers outside their comfort zone, especially when there is a personal relationship between the employee and the manager.

- **Risky** – There is certainly a high degree of risk when tackling a poor performer. Heated arguments, accusations of bullying, even being criticised by the company when things go wrong, all add to the risk.

Because managers find poor performance management complicated, uncomfortable, unpleasant, and risky, many managers just 'maintain the status quo' because it is much safer and easier to do so.

Reluctance

'Unwillingness or disinclination to do something necessary or important'

What is the solution?

A good starting point

Apart from 'cheque book' management, there is no 'quick fix' solution to resolving poor performance issues, however implementing the following strategy will have the immediate effect of improving performance within an organisation.

Step 1 – Put poor performance on the corporate agenda

Executives should promote 'the correct performance' as a company **value** and instill this value throughout the organisation.

Step 2 – Measure and Monitor employee performance

Audit values on a regular basis, analyse results and ensure the right corrective action is being taken where issues are identified.

Step 3 – Review effectiveness of poor performance procedures

Poor performance procedures need to be clearly understood by all, manageable, and not complicated.

Step 4 – Support managers when they tackle poor performance

Managing a poor performance issue well is difficult: when managers make mistakes treat them as 'learning opportunities' rather than an opportunity to criticise them.

Step 5 – Learn from every incident
Organisations/managers must learn from incidents and mistakes.

Every appeal, grievance and tribunal claim is an opportunity for learning and development for all managers, support services and executives within an organisation.

Corporate Agenda

'An Executive list, plan, outline of things to be achieved, in order to improve overall business performance'

Chapter 2
Critical Learning

'Everybody is born with an L plate on their back; when they die, it is still there – just a little smaller'

Chapter 2 – Critical Learning

- Employers have rights too!

- Employment Legislation

- ACAS Code of Practice

- 'Fair and Reasonable' explained

- Objectives Management

- Performance Management

- Communicating Assertively

- The Method and Manner Approach

Employers have rights too!

I remember it well ……

I was conducting a very challenging disciplinary interview in a large retail distribution centre. The employee I was disciplining was constantly failing to achieve his productivity targets and consistently turned up for work late, and when he was approached about this by his Line Manager he became argumentative and aggressive.

At the disciplinary meeting the employee was represented by a very assertive union representative who, with careful and clever questioning, took me off track, tied me up in red tape and made me feel incompetent in the handling of a disciplinary interview. Throughout the interview both the union rep and employee repeatedly said "We know our rights!" Just on the verge of losing control of the interview altogether and looking stupid, I replied "Managers have rights too you know! Every Manager has a right to ask employees to do the job they are paid to do, turn up for work when they are meant to and behave appropriately whilst at work. The facts are clear – this employee is infringing our rights in all three of these areas!"

With that comment there was a sudden 'back tracking' by both the union rep and the employee as they were pushed on to the back foot and had to defend themselves rather than attack me. Observing this, my confidence improved considerably and I was able to regain control of the meeting. The employee was issued with a formal warning for poor performance, poor attendance and unacceptable behaviour. The employee did not appeal.

Mantra

**'A word or phrase that is often
repeated, which expresses
a particular strong belief'**

Everybody has rights:

Employees have many rights – they are well protected and the amount and complexity of employment legislation is mind-boggling. What a great many employers, managers, and employees are overlooking is the fact that employers have employment rights too.

Every employer has a right to ask their employees to: do the job they are paid to do as outlined in the job description **(Performance)**, behave appropriately whilst at work **(Behaviour)** and turn up for work when they are meant to **(Attendance)**.

No employee, union representative, employment law advisor or tribunal can argue with these basic facts. However, achieving these basic employer rights without infringing the employment rights of the employee certainly is challenging, but if you continually remind yourself of this and – when required – remind your employees of this fact, few performance issues will arise, and if they do, they will be resolved at an early stage.

Every Manager's Mantra

'Every Manager has a right to ask employees to: do the job they are paid to do, behave appropriately whilst at work and turn up for work when they are meant to'

Employment Legislation

Disciplinary and Dismissal Legislation – there is none now!

Managers know their 'products' in great detail, but very often do not know the specific 'HR' aspects of their role. Many Managers make mistakes and get into difficulties when tackling poor performance issues simply because they do not have a basic understanding of Employment Legislation.

Compulsory Dispute Resolution Procedures Legislation pre April 2009

The Compulsory 'Dispute Resolution' Procedures introduced in October 2004 stated that if an employer did not follow the mandatory **'three-step'** process when disciplining or dismissing an employee, this would <u>automatically</u> be deemed to be an unfair dismissal. The three-step rule was quite clear:

Step 1 – Notification in writing

Step 2 – Meeting

Step 3 – Appeal

Because these compulsory "dispute resolution" procedural rules proved to be unsatisfactory and counter-productive in resolving work based disputes, **the rule was scrapped with effect from 6th April 2009.** What this meant was that Tribunals could now make judgments on

'fair and reasonable' actions taken by an employer rather than be bound by the compulsory three-step rule. Although there is now no 'Law' governing the handling of Dismissal and Disciplinary disputes, that does not mean Employers can do what they want when resolving performance issues, because the mandatory procedures have been replaced by the semi-voluntary **ACAS Code of Practice.**

Employment Legislation

'The area of Law that covers all aspects of employer and employee relationships'

ACAS Code of Practice

ACAS Code of Practice on Disciplinary and Grievance Procedures

The Code is basically the same as the former mandatory **three-step rule:**

Step 1 – <u>Notification in writing</u> of a disciplinary meeting.

Step 2 – <u>Conduct a meeting,</u> giving the employee the opportunity to be accompanied and to be able to present mitigating circumstances.

Step 3 – Give the employee the opportunity to <u>Appeal</u> if they are dissatisfied with the outcome of the disciplinary meeting.

Employer's responsibilities

Employers do not have to work to this Code but they should because – apart from being professional and fair – if an employee dispute does go to a Tribunal and the employer loses the case (and if it is found that the employer did not adhere to the three-step rule) any compensation awarded to the employee may be increased by up to 25%.

Employee's responsibilities

The ACAS Code **applies to the employee also,** because if the employee did not adhere to the Code e.g. they walked off the job or did not appeal against a sanction given, any compensation they are awarded may be <u>reduced by</u> 25%.

Many employees and employers believe that whatever ACAS says, the employer **has** to do, however ACAS is **advisory** only. Employers can do whatever they want to do when it comes to a disciplinary/dismissal situation, but they do have to justify that their actions were 'fair and reasonable' if brought before a Tribunal.

ACAS

Advisory, Conciliation and Arbitration Service 'Improving organisations and working life through better employment relations'

'Fair and Reasonable' explained

What is Fair and Reasonable?

Although disciplinary or dismissal disputes are now judged on Fair and Reasonable actions by the employer, there is a great deal of confusion as to what is meant by **'Fair and Reasonable'**.

If you can demonstrate that you have covered the following 7 key areas, you should be reasonably safe from any unfair or unreasonable tribunal claims by an employee.

1. There was clear <u>evidence</u> of poor performance.
2. The employee was <u>made aware</u> of the exact nature of the concerns.
3. It was made clear to the employee the standard of performance that was <u>expected.</u>
4. Appropriate <u>training/support</u> was provided to the employee to help them improve.
5. The employee was given <u>adequate time to improve.</u>
6. It was made clear to the employee the <u>potential consequences</u> of failing to achieve the required standard of performance.
7. All employees in the organisation are <u>treated in the same way.</u>

Incorporating the **Fair and Reasonable Charter** into the employee's contract of employment/handbook would be an effective way of letting people know where they stand, and minimising disputes when a disciplinary or dismissal situation occurs.

See Fair and Reasonable Charter – Appendix 2

Fair and Reasonable

'Free from bias, dishonesty, or injustice and the standard of care that a reasonably prudent person would observe under a given set of circumstances'

Objectives Management

Management by Objectives (or **MBO** as it is typically called) is not a management fad. Organisations have objectives, managers work to objectives, managers have to set objectives and managers are nearly always measured on the achievement of objectives.

MBO is particularly important to managers when having to tackle poor performance. Set an employee some objectives to improve performance or behaviour and you have covered a crucial step because, by definition, this means the poor performance issue exists. If the employee does not dispute the objectives they are being issued with, then they are effectively admitting they are under-performing.

Objective linked improvement plans.

An objective is simply 'a Task or Target with a deadline' and many managers think that just setting the right objectives will produce the required result. Every objective set should have a list of the 'actions required' to achieve the objective: i.e. Action plans. This is critical 'poor performance' management, because it is the action plans that will be reviewed rather than the objective.

Paper Trail

Employees need to know 'what to do' if they are going to achieve the required standard. The setting of clear objectives, and agreeing with the employee the actions required to achieve them, is the crucial step in the performance management process. It is vital because the objectives and action plans will be a key part of the paper trail if an issue needs to be taken to the next, formal level.

Objective
'A specific result that a person aims to achieve within a specific timeframe'

Performance Management

Performance Management Explained

Mention the phrase Performance Management to many employees or managers and they will immediately think negatively. Some will view performance management as 'Disciplinary'; others will view it as 'Appraisal' or 'Review'. Performance Management is in fact **EVERYTHING** a manager does, and knowing which 'tool' to use and which process to follow is essential if a manager is going to be effective in managing performance (thus: Performance Management).

Every manager needs to be aware of (and practiced in) the use of the following, as they are specific to 'correcting' performance.

Procedures

- Company operating procedures
- Job descriptions
- Induction procedures
- Continuous improvement procedures
- Disciplinary & Grievance and Appeal procedures

Techniques

- The Performance Management cycle
- Objectives Management
- The Method and Manner Track
- The GRASPING the Nettle Process

The Performance Management 'Tool Kit' Audit
Audit yourself and/or your organisation by asking how well you use these tools in managing Employee Performance.

See Performance Management Tool Kit – Appendix 3

Performance Management

'The practice of using tools, procedures and techniques to develop, correct or reward performance'

Communicating Assertively

Assertiveness

Assertiveness is basically a communication technique that needs to be used by managers when dealing with confrontational issues such as poor performance or poor behaviour. It is a method of communicating your rights as a manager without infringing the rights of the employee. It is something that every manager needs to learn and continually develop if they are to survive as managers.

Communicating Assertively

Giving employees feedback on their poor performance is not easy, it can be unpleasant and there is also a degree of risk. That is why many managers avoid doing it – or when they do, they lose their cool, get all emotional and say all the wrong things. This often results in 'undefendable' accusations of bullying. Stick to the following 'behaviours' and you will not only get your message across, but you will be able to defend any accusation of bullying also.

Some good behaviours of the assertive manager

- Be direct, don't soft pedal and don't go around the houses.
- Don't show your emotions – act, pretend, hide them.
- Don't raise your voice in any way – keep the pitch low and level.

- Apologise immediately if you say anything wrong or out of place.
- Don't use aggressive hand gestures.
- Have a relaxed and composed manner – do not display aggressive body language.
- Don't threaten - if necessary, spell out the consequences.
- Don't use words that will provoke a hostile or defensive response.
- Communicate in the same way to all employees.
- Finish all conversations on a positive note.

Assertive
'Confident and direct in claiming one's rights or putting one's views across'

The Method & Manner Approach

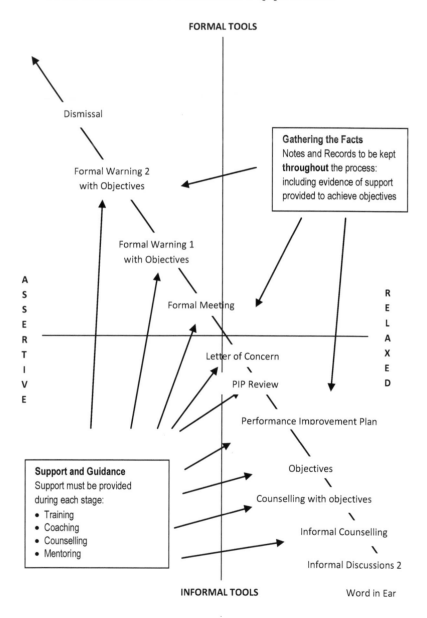

FORMAL TOOLS

Dismissal

Formal Warning 2
with Objectives

Gathering the Facts
Notes and Records to be kept
throughout the process:
including evidence of support
provided to achieve objectives

Formal Warning 1
with Objectives

A
S
S
E
R
T
I
V
E

R
E
L
A
X
E
D

Formal Meeting

Letter of Concern

PIP Review

Performance Improvement Plan

Support and Guidance
Support must be provided
during each stage:
• Training
• Coaching
• Counselling
• Mentoring

Objectives

Counselling with objectives

Informal Counselling

Informal Discussions 2

INFORMAL TOOLS   Word in Ear

Method and Manner

Managing poor performance is all about **Method** (the tools used) and **Manner** (the style with which you use the tools). In the early stages of dealing with poor performance, managers should take an informal (almost 'relaxed') approach to resolving it. Conversations should be casual and the tools used should be informal such as on-feet discussions.

If improvement is not quickly apparent, managers should then use a little more formality (such as an office chat) and become a little more assertive in their communication.

If there is still no improvement, managers should gradually move towards the more formal tools at their disposal (Disciplinary Meetings) and their style has to become more assertive in their use.

Using a sledgehammer to crack a nut

Very often managers have a 'knee jerk' reaction and go straight for the more formal tools (PIPs, Disciplinary Meetings,) which can be viewed as overly aggressive in style.

Gross-misconduct

The Method and Manner approach is only a guide: more serious situations will require the immediate use of formal tools and the manager will need to be quickly assertive in style.

Chapter 3

5 things you must do every time

Priority
'Something that is regarded as more important than another'

5 things you must do every time

1. Gather the facts

2. Deal with issues quickly

3. Get confirmation that the issue exists

4. Write things down

5. Use a PIP <u>before</u> taking formal action

1 Gather the Facts

You cannot do anything without clear facts

Without facts you will not be able to present a viable case when you have the inevitable discussion with the employee. Facts can be gathered by analysing results, statistics, records and non-achievements. You can also gather facts through observation and feedback from others.

As you gather the facts, a picture will form as to whether the problem is a 'performance issue' or a 'behaviour' one. Very often this exercise will confirm what you thought (or already knew) but this exercise will certainly help you to concentrate your thoughts, identify the 'big issues' and plan the right actions.

Aide-memoire List (Memory Aid)

The best way to gather the facts is to use a memory aid: - nothing complicated or time consuming, just somewhere to list key words, dates, events etc. that will prompt your memory about a certain situation. The most effective aide-memoire list is to find a blank page in your diary, draw a line down the centre of the page and record all of the negative instances of this employee's performance on one side and the positive aspects on the other.

Recording the positive aspects of an employee's performance is just as important as recording negative ones, because you need to take a balanced view of someone's performance, and you will need to be able to say some positive things when you have your discussion with him/her.

See example Aide-Memoire list - Appendix 4

Facts
'A thing that is indisputably the case'

2. Deal with issues quickly

'People problems' do not normally go away on their own, and the longer you leave them the more difficult they are to sort out.

Probationary periods

It is a fact that many poor performing employees have <u>always</u> performed below the required standard. Their poor performance or poor behaviour existed right from the beginning of their employment. The problem exists **now** because the probationary period 'tool' was not used effectively or decisively by the manager 'in situ' at the time of their appointment. This knowledge is not a great deal of use to you in the resolving of your particular issue(s) but it is an important message with regards to employing new people and in the use of probationary periods.

Letting employees know that you know

If you have inherited poor performance, it is important that you deal with the problems quickly and decisively. Just letting poor performing employees 'know that you know' that they are performing below the required standard and that 'you are quite prepared' to discuss the issue with them, will have a positive influence both on the employee and the overall performance of the team.

Long-term performance issues
Just because a long-term employee has always performed badly does not mean that it is too late to do something about it. Call the employee to one side and say; "enough is enough," apologise for not saying something earlier, and ask them to improve their performance/behaviour 'as from now'.

Procrastination
'The practice of carrying out less urgent tasks in preference to more urgent ones, thus putting off impending tasks to a later time'

3. Get confirmation that the issue exists

Confirming the problem exists
It is vitally important that you get confirmation that the problem actually exists, and getting the employee to agree to do something about it is a major step forward.

You do not need to say outright "you are under-performing aren't you", you can gain confirmation the problem exists in more subtle ways.

Stating facts, offering support
Simply stating the facts and saying "how can I help resolve this issue?" is an easy way of gaining confirmation, because just going into discussion about the situation and agreeing some important improvement actions will in itself be the confirmation you need.

Getting confirmation that the issue exists is also important in the event of having to defend your actions in the event of a complaint against you (Grievance). Many grievances against the line manager are the direct result of a discussion on poor performance. If you have already confirmed the poor performance issue exists, the employee can only complain about your style and not what you were saying or trying to achieve.

Poor performing employees do not like having to admit they are not performing to the required standard but when you get them to, this is a big step in getting improvement.

Confirmation
'Establishing the truth or correctness of something believed or suspected to be the case.'

4. Write things down

The pen is certainly mightier than the sword as writing has more influence on people and events than the use of verbal communication. Many managers underestimate the importance of the written word and do not put pen to paper when it is necessary. There are a number of important benefits from writing things down:-

Paper trail

Written communication, such as memos, summaries of discussions, minutes of meetings, and appraisal/review documentation all form an important 'paper trail' of events. The more documentation you have, the easier it is to progress to more formal discussions (should the need arise).

Getting someone's attention

With the more challenging employee, it is sometimes difficult to get their attention. These employees feel you are not serious and you will go away in time. Issuing an employee with some type of written communication has a very impactful effect on getting their attention. Sometimes positive (often negative!!) but doing this will give a clear message: 'this is serious and I am not letting you get away with it'.

Letter of concern

Some managers entitle memos/letters 'Letter of Concern' to add impact to the message, but too much use of this 'tool' and it will lose its impact. Letters of Concern should really be a last resort and used as the link between informal and formal action (not in every instance).

Notes and Records

'A brief record of facts written down to aid memory kept - together with information set down in writing - as a means of evidence'

5. Use a PIP <u>before</u> taking formal action

Nearly all procedures relating to disciplinary and dismissal procedures promote the use of a Performance Improvement Plan (PIP) being issued <u>following</u> a disciplinary warning being given. Issuing the PIP <u>before</u> moving into a formal meeting is far more effective and impactful.

What is a Performance Improvement Plan (PIP)?
A PIP outlines the performance and/or behaviours that need to be improved and the actions that will be required to enable the employee to meet the required standard. A well written PIP will:

- Specifically identify the performance to be improved or the behaviour to be corrected
- Provide clear instructions/descriptions relating to the work that is to be performed or behaviour that needs to change
- Outline the support that will be provided to achieve the plan
- Clearly communicate the agreed review dates and process
- Spell out the <u>consequences</u> if performance or behaviour standards are not met

The PIP is <u>the</u> most important document in the event of having to defend a Tribunal claim. A clearly written Performance Improvement Plan is a powerful defence document because it confirms the poor performance issue exists and shows that the organisation has tried to improve performance. A constructive dismissal claim will be very difficult to prove when a concise/clearly worded PIP has been issued.

See Example PIP – Appendix 5

Performance Improvement Plan (PIP)
'A clear and detailed written plan relating to the work that is to be performed or the behaviour that needs to change'.

Chapter 4

5 Important tools for managing poor performance

Performance
''The accomplishment of a given task measured against known standards of: accuracy, completeness, cost or speed'

5 important tools for managing poor performance

1. Poor Performance Procedures

2. Job descriptions

3. Probationary periods

4. Reviews and Appraisals

5. Performance Improvement Plans

1. Poor Performance Procedures

All organisations have disciplinary procedures written into the contract of employment, but these tend to outline the stages of formal disciplinary sanctions rather than step by step procedures for managers to work to. There are a great deal of things a manager needs to do <u>before</u> moving to a formal discussion, but few organisations clearly outline what these informal actions are and the procedures that managers need to follow. If organisations outlined informal/semi-informal procedures in the employee contract/handbook and incorporated these procedures into the manager's operating procedures, then there would be fewer arguments and far fewer complaints.

Informal procedures

Step 1 – Gather the facts and identify the big issue

Step 2 – Manager sits down with employee, discusses issues and agrees improvement plans and review dates

Step 3 – Employee implements plan with the support of manager

Step 4 – Manager/employee review progress and manager provides additional support if employee struggling.

Semi-formal procedures

Step 5 – Manager to issue employee with Performance Improvement Plan (PIP) and outline consequences for not working to the plan

Step 6 – Manager to provide appropriate training/ coaching/support

Step 7 – Manager/employee to review progress on a weekly basis.

See Example: Poor Performance Procedures – Appendix 7

Procedures
'A clear series of steps taken to accomplish an end result, for all to follow'

2. Job Descriptions

It is important that all employees are issued with a job description before they start a job. This should be separate from the employment contract. The job description is the contract they have with the employer and failure to achieve what is outlined in the job description is a breach of contract on the employee's part.

The problem with job descriptions

Many job descriptions are written badly; they can be vague, inflexible and not specific to the job. Job descriptions are rarely referred to once an employee has started employment – unless, that is, the employee has an issue with their job!!

Job descriptions need to be written in a format that will clearly outline what an employee needs to achieve within a job, and in a format that will help managers 'manage performance' more effectively.

The 'Appraisable and Objective settable' job description

Objective-based job descriptions outline what an employee is expected to <u>achieve</u> rather than what they are expected to <u>do</u> within the job. An objectives based job description is also far more effective when assessing an employee's performance (both periodically <u>and</u> during their annual appraisal) but, it is also far more useful for identifying relevant performance/improvement objectives when an employee is not reaching the standard of performance required.

See Example: Objectives based Job Description – Appendix 6

Employment Contract

'A written agreement specifying terms and conditions under which an employee consents to perform, in return for an agreed wage or salary'

3. Probationary Periods

The **probationary period** and the facility to be able to extend probationary periods when deemed necessary, is a vital and valuable 'performance management tool'.

Induction Objectives

Many under-performers within the workplace today were probably under-performing from the very beginning and have never really performed to the required standard. All employees, whether they are managers or front line team members, should start off their employment with a defined set of Induction Objectives clearly outlining what they are expected to have achieved, learnt or developed within the probationary period.

These objectives can then be reviewed on a regular basis and if they are not being achieved (or little effort has been put into achieving them by the employee) then an employer has every right to extend the probationary period or ask the employee to leave the organisation.

All too often organisations hastily give new employees permanent contracts without reviewing their performance/behaviour during the initial probationary period.

See Example: Induction Objectives Appendices 8/9

Probation Period

'A process or period in which an employee's suitability is assessed and for an employee to assess suitability of an organisation'

4. Reviews and Appraisals

Performance Reviews

Regular performance reviews are an important tool of performance management. Periodic reviews of an employee's objectives are an important duty for all managers. It is no good waiting until the end of the annual review to pour out a list of performance concerns that have been ongoing throughout the year. Quarterly and/or mid-year objectives reviews need to be conducted appropriately. A good performer would probably only need one or two reviews during the year, whereas an under-performer needs to have their performance reviewed more frequently. Performance reviews are crucial to improving performance on a rapid basis.

Annual Appraisals

Many managers view the annual appraisal as time consuming and an unnecessary administration exercise. However, appraisals have now become a critical tool for improving performance. The annual appraisal is an opportunity to review the person's performance in relation to the job description and identify areas for improvement, if there are any shortfalls in performance. If the reviews throughout the year have been well conducted, there should be no surprises, and the annual appraisal would capture and summarise the person's performance throughout the review period. Too often an employee's appraisal contradicts a manager's verbal view of an employee's performance, and this can hinder the appropriate course of action being taken.

See Example: Appraisal (Poor Performer) – Appendix 10

Performance Appraisal
'The process by which a manager evaluates an employee's work performance and behaviour'

5. Performance Improvement Plans

As mentioned in Chapter 3, in the case of consistent poor performance, issuing an employee with a Performance Improvement Plan (PIP) is an important activity <u>prior</u> to moving into any disciplinary process.

What is a Performance Improvement Plan?

The Performance Improvement Plan is basically a list of performance improving objectives and a <u>plan of activities</u> for achieving them. It would still be classed as 'informal' at this stage, but employees should be made fully aware that not achieving or not putting sufficient effort into achieving the objectives, will result in the matter being referred to a disciplinary interview.

The reason why the employee is being given a Performance Improvement Plan should be made very clear. It must be objectives-based so the employee knows what they have to achieve in order to bring them to the required standard of performance, and what will happen if they fail to achieve what is expected of them. To ensure fairness, employers must give the employee as much help, support, training and so forth, as is necessary to reach the required standards.

The PIP is the key link between informal and formal discussions and is the last step of the informal process. If you get to this stage, you are probably going to have to go the whole disciplinary route.

See Example: Performance Improvement Plan - Appendix 5

Performance Improvement Plan
'The key link between informal
and formal discussions'

Chapter 5

5 Important tools for managing poor behaviour

Behaviour
'Actions taken and mannerisms displayed by people in conjunction with their environment'

5 Important tools for managing poor behaviour

1. Company Values

2. Employee Handbook

3. Personal Improvement Plans

4. Letter of Concern

5. The Disciplinary Interview

1. Company Values

Resolving poor behaviour issues is certainly more challenging than managing poor performance. Whereas poor performance can be managed with the job description, managers need to manage poor behaviour using a different 'tool' and that tool is: Company Values.

About Company Values

All employees are required to conduct themselves in a manner that is consistent with the values of the organisation, but many organisations do not have a defined set of Company Values for employees to work to or for managers to instill. Even if you work in an organisation where Company values have not been defined, there are still certain values that do not need to be written down – these are normal behaviours that every employee should work to. It is **fair and reasonable** for employers to expect their employees to be:

- Dependable, Reliable
- Respectful
- Punctual
- Supportive
- Caring of others
- Motivated

When an employee behaves contrary to these values there will be damage to the business/team performance: therefore every manager has a right and duty to talk to the employee about it. Values do not drive the business; they drive the people within the business.

See Example: Company Values – Appendix 11

Company Values

'Principles, standards or qualities considered worthwhile or desirable to an organisation'

2. Employee Handbook

An employee handbook (sometimes known as the employee manual) is a booklet normally issued to an employee by the employer. Usually the employee handbook contains information about company policies and procedures. This generally includes:

- Welcome statement
- Holiday booking procedures
- Hours of work
- Health and welfare information
- Disciplinary and dismissal procedures

When written carefully, the employee handbook can be culture influencing with regards to poor performance, as it is the perfect tool for communicating company expectations regarding performance or behaviour. To support the managers in poor performance management, all handbooks need to include: –

- Company Values – reviews and on-ongoing assessments
- Sickness benefits – procedures in the event of abuse
- Performance management information – reviews & appraisals
- Poor performance Procedure – PIPs, disciplinary
- Punctuality – standards and expectations.

Having these specific areas highlighted in the handbook would in itself have a positive effect on poor performance within an organisation.

Employee Handbook
'A powerful culture influencing tool, communicating expectations relating to conduct and behaviour within the workplace'

3. Personal Improvement Plan

Personal Improvement Plan – still a PIP

Putting together improvement plans relating to poor performance is relatively easy; putting an improvement plan together relating to someone's behaviour is a bit trickier. The reason for this is that managers have a right to ask for immediate improvement in behaviour, therefore 'stop doing it' is the only action you can put down. However, if the employee is issued a Personal Improvement Plan outlining some alternative actions, this will help in the monitoring and reviewing of the plan.

Argumentative behaviour – discuss issues with manager in private, not in front of other employees.

Aggressive behaviour towards other team members – bring issues to the attention of the manager before he/she has to try and resolve them.

Issuing an employee with a Personal Improvement Plan will serve three main purposes: -

1. A wake-up call: it lets the employee know that you are not prepared to tolerate their poor behaviour.

2. A clearly outlined 'reviewable' list of actions for the employee to work to in order for them to achieve the required standard.

3. An important part of the paper trail you will need to put together in the event of you referring matters to a disciplinary interview.

See Example: Personal Improvement Plan – Appendix 12

Personal Improvement Plan
'A structured and supported process undertaken by an individual to improve behaviour'

4. Letter of Concern

What is a letter of concern?

Very simply, it is a personal letter/memorandum that has the words **Letter of Concern** at the top of the page.

This is purposely done to add impact to the letter and to make the employee aware of the seriousness of the situation.

It is normally issued after an <u>informal</u> meeting with an employee when disciplinary action is not necessary at the time.

The letter should:

- Confirm that a discussion has taken place: day, date, venue etc.
- Briefly outline the discussion points/concerns
- Confirm timescales within which the improvement is required
- State the consequences (Formal action) in the event of continued poor performance/behaviour.

Best use of the Letter of Concern

Best use of this tool is when you have reviewed the employee's PIP and found there is insufficient improvement in the required performance. It should be used as the very last resort before moving on to formal discussions.

Paper trail

The letter of concern is also a valuable addition to the paper trail that will need to be amassed in preparation for formal procedures.

See Example: Letter of Concern – Appendix 13

Letter of Concern

'To be used following an informal meeting with an employee to highlight a concern, but when disciplinary action is not necessary'

5. The Disciplinary Interview

The disciplinary interview in itself is a very effective tool for improving poor performance/behaviour but only when it is used correctly and in a timely fashion. If you have done all the ground work, i.e. performance improvement plans, letter of concern and so forth, and no improvement has been achieved, the employee has given you little choice other than to go down the more formal route. Make sure you communicate that fact.

The disciplinary interview – the overall purpose of the disciplinary interview is to 'decide' what to do, which means managers have a choice to not issue a warning if they don't want to, using the employee's attendance at the disciplinary interview as a 'message' in itself. Concluding a disciplinary interview with "I am not issuing you with a formal warning at this stage, but there will be a 'note on file' that this interview took place," can be extremely effective.

Technical Point
Many managers (and advisors) think that they cannot conduct a disciplinary interview without a formal 'fact finding' taking place, and that the person who conducts the disciplinary interview should not be the same person who conducted the fact finding. This is absolutely the

correct procedure for potential **gross misconduct issues**, i.e. an issue that could lead to a dismissal. However, with minor instances of poor performance/behaviour, it is quite acceptable for a manager to gather facts and information and conduct and present these facts at a disciplinary interview. Also see ACAS procedures.

Disciplinary Interview
'A formal discussion to determine a suitable course of action'

Chapter 6

5 important tools for managing poor attendance

Attendance

'The action of going to or being present at a place or event'

5 important tools for managing poor attendance

1. Absence Procedures

2. Notes and Records

3. The Bradford Factor

4. The Return to Work interview

5. The Self-Certification Form

1. Absence Procedures

Absence Procedures

If you look at organisations that <u>do not</u> have absence issues, you will normally find they have a clear set of procedures which are understood by all employees, and a robust approach to line managers who do not implement them. This approach has **created a culture** where all employees know that regular attendance is expected, and that irregular attendance will not be accepted. Absence procedures should be communicated to employees via the employee handbook and should include:–

- Clear procedures relating to reporting absence
- Return to work procedures which include details of the manager's responsibilities
- Clear communication relating to monitoring absence
- Procedures when excessive absence occurs
- A reminder to employees that sick pay is a benefit which can be withdrawn if the company feels it is appropriate.

Absence procedures should also have clear operating procedures for line managers to work to when there is a need to address poor attendance. These procedures should include:–

- Mandatory procedures relating to recording of absence
- Procedures relating to 'Return to Work' interviews
- Procedures relating to unsatisfactory absence
- Sanctions that a manager can apply where appropriate.

Absence Procedures
'A process to influence a Culture where regular attendance is expected rather than irregular attendance being accepted'

2. Notes and Records

There will always be employees who take the odd 'sickie' day, and managers would be foolish if they thought they could stop this. Most of these employees however do not take full advantage of the company sick pay benefits, but unfortunately there are others who do. These employees cause the most disruption to business. Many managers feel there is little that can be done to stop this happening, but keeping records and letting the employee know you are keeping records, is an effective psychological way of reducing the amount of 'sickies' these employees take. The two key notes and records managers need to maintain are Attendance Records and Self Certification forms.

Attendance Records – Every employee should have records of attendance in their personnel file. All absence – holidays, sick days, non-working days should be recorded on one document. If an employee is trying to take advantage of company sick pay benefits, then this document will reveal this very quickly.

Self-certification forms – Many managers overlook the importance of this document. As well as assisting organisations in maintaining Statutory Sick Pay regulations, it is also a useful document for managers to analyse and discuss. This form has three important pieces of information – 1. Reason for sickness, 2. Whether a doctor has been seen, and 3. the employee's signature. Each of these are important details when conducting 'the return to work' interview.

See Example: Sickness Record – Appendix 14

Absence Records
'Gathered factual absence information for analysis, problem solving and action planning'

3. The Bradford Factor

Very often the amount of sick days an employee takes is seen as the measure of absenteeism. This is not very accurate because it does not take into consideration long term absence. An employee taking a single longer term period of absence would be seen as having a poor sickness record, whereas an employee who takes repeated one-off sick days would not. It is employees who take short, frequent and unplanned periods of absence that damage the business most, and is where the main focus for improvement should be directed.

The Bradford Factor
The Bradford Factor addresses this problem by measuring the <u>amount of instances</u> an employee is off sick rather than the <u>amount of days</u> an employee has been absent.

Example
One instance of absence of 10 days would result in a Bradford Factor score of only <u>10 points</u>. Whereas 5 instances of absence, each of two days, would result in a Bradford Factor score of <u>250 points.</u>

The Bradford Factor is an excellent tool for identifying potential abuse of an organisation's sick pay benefits.

See full explanation of the Bradford Factor – Appendix 15

The Bradford Factor
Instances of absence multiplied by total amount of days = S^2
Total number of days taken over a period = D

S^2 x D = Bradford Factor

4. The Return to Work interview

The Return to Work meeting is to enable the employee to share concerns with the manager about their illness, and their general state of health in relation to their job. This meeting is essential in monitoring absence accurately and reinforcing the message that the organisation cares about employee sickness absence.

If the employee is rarely off sick, the meeting is likely to be brief. However, should an employee return to work after a succession of frequent, intermittent absences or after long term absence, the interview will be much more structured.

The purpose of the return to work interview is to:

- See how the member of staff is on their return to work, and ensure they are fit to do so
- Establish the cause of absence and, where appropriate, discuss it further.

If the employee has been away for a period of seven days or more, they are required to provide a 'Fit' (previously 'Sick') note. There is always a requirement to discuss details to ensure the employee does not require any adjustments to their working environment on their return to work.

Return to work interview

'An opportunity for an employee to share concerns about their illness and general state of health in relation to their job'

5. The Self-Certification Form

When you know you are dealing with an employee who is taking advantage of your organisation's sickness benefits, the Self-Certification form is a powerful tool to indirectly let the employee know that you know what they are doing.

With analysis completed, self-certification will give you three significant points to consider and discuss with the employee:-

1. Reasons for absence – This needs to be looked at closely to see if there is a pattern of similar sickness reasons. If there is, then you can ask the employee to contact their doctor for details. If there is not, this is a good indication that this employee may be taking advantage.

2. Has this employee consulted a Doctor? – If this employee has not contacted a Doctor on any occasion, then this again is a good indication that this employee may be taking advantage.

3. The Employee Signature – What many employees overlook is that the self-certification form is a formal document and falsifying information on it could be viewed as a gross-misconduct situation.

A good test of an employee's honesty is, during the Return to Work interview, ask the employee why they were off sick on a certain date. If they <u>were</u> sick they should easily remember; if they were not sick they will probably have forgotten what reason they gave at the time or wrote down on the self-certification form.

See Example: Self Certification Form – Appendix 16

Self-Certification Form
'A formal document to assist organisations in the management of Statutory Sickness'

Chapter 7

GRASPING the Nettle –

Taking action immediately in order to deal with a difficult or unpleasant situation

Where to start, what to do

Where to start

Where to start, what to do.

Many managers are at a loss where to start and what to do when having to confront a performance or behaviour issue, so here is a sequence that will not only get you started but will also give you a step by step guide to follow.

Mnemonic
'A pattern of letters that assists in remembering something important or significant'

The GRASPING the Nettle Process

Step 1 – **G**ather the facts

Step 2 – **R**eview the facts and identify the big issues

Step 3 – **A**rrange and plan a meeting

Step 4 – **S**it down and discuss the big issues

Step 5 – **P**ut together an agreed action plan

Step 6 – **I**nform others of what you have done

Step 7 – **N**otate everything!

Step 8 – **G**et ready for some fallout

Aide-Memoire Notes

Gathering the Facts

'Gathering information on what has really occurred or is actually the case'

Step 1 – **G**ather the Facts

As covered in Chapter 3, you cannot do or say anything without clear facts to refer to, so this is the critical starting point in the process.

Aide memoire notes
Find a blank page in your diary, put the employee's initials at the top of the page, draw a line down the middle and put a ☺ on one side and a ☹ on the other. List all occurrences where the employee has performed/behaved below the required standard under the column. Just write down key words/dates, this is just a memory jogger (aide-memoire note) and not a list of crimes to attack them with.

You will have to talk to the employee at some stage, so to make the discussion more constructive and objective (non-personal) list as many <u>positive</u> things about this person's performance/behaviour under the ☺ column. If you cannot think of anything positive – try harder!

Best practice
Managers should do this with each of their employees as it is professional HR management, and will assist in conducting fair and reasonable reviews & appraisal.

Analysing the Facts

Review
'To assess a situation with the intention of implementing necessary change'

Positive points:
01/4 - Good quality of work completed on a specific project
11/6 - Trained new team members in H&S
14/8 - Sorted a problem out no other could sort

Attendance Issues:
4/4 - Late for work
14/4 - Late for work (missed bus)
12/5 - Did not turn in, no notification (Mon)
14/5 - Sick migraine (Fri)
27/5 - Sick stomach problems (Fri)

Behaviour Issues:
11/4 - Argued with team members over trivial matter
14/5 - Rude and aggressive to new team member
22/6 – Refused to support colleague during busy period
14/8 - Rude and aggressive towards customer
27/9 - Argued in front of other team members

Performance Issues:
11/4 - Missed deadline
14/5 - Errors in administration that caused considerable disruption
23/6 - Late in finishing project
14/7 - Late in finishing project
27/9 - Takes longer to complete tasks than newer employees (3 occasions)

Step 2 – Review the facts and identify the big issues

Analysing the facts

You probably already know what the big issue(s) is/are; this step will help you to confirm them. In your analysis, do not focus on one-off instances because they are easy to defend. Identify the repeat issues, the indefensible facts that will require an explanation rather than a denial. Wait until you have a minimum of three identical/ similar issues to present to the employee. It will be very difficult for an employee to defend something that has happened on three separate occasions.

This analysis will also identify whether the problem is a performance or behaviour issue. Poor performance is normally correctable with training and coaching, behaviour issues will require counselling and mentoring support.

Important note:

If an employee has achieved the required standard previously, then the issue needs to be treated as poor 'behaviour' rather than poor 'performance'.

Planning & Preparing

Knee Jerk Reaction
'An immediate, reflex reaction made without thought, analysis or planning'

Check List

- Will you have enough facts? ☐
- Have you identified the big issues? ☐
- Is the meeting venue suitable?
  - Will you be interrupted? ☐
  - Is it privates, will anybody over here? ☐
- Have you planned enough time? ☐
- Have you structured your discussion? ☐
- Have you prepared your opening comments? ☐
- Are you prepared for their response? ☐
- Are you in the right frame of mind? ☐

Step 3 – Arrange and plan a meeting

Do not go into a discussion without planning it first!
Nothing will get resolved without a discussion, so you need to plan:
- When will you hold it?
- Where will you hold it?
- What are you going to say?
- How are you going to say it?

Good preparation will give you confidence and control if needed. If you are unsure in any way get some performance management coaching!

When you discuss the issue(s) you are technically conducting an <u>informal</u> counselling meeting. If you have a third party attending the discussion, it could be seen as a <u>formal</u> discussion which technically means the employee has a right to be accompanied also. Keep initial discussions informal.

Important point:
Don't plan to hold this discussion outside the office (pub/coffee shop) as this could be misconstrued. Don't hold the employee back at the end of the day – this is business, so do it in business time on business premises.

Giving Feedback

Feedback
'Communicating progress and achievement information as a basis for improvement or recognition'

Tell, Sell, Discuss

Performance

Tell: "Peter, I need to talk to you about your performance, in the past few weeks you have missed some important deadlines and you have made numerous document errors." (Facts from Aide Memoir list)

Sell: "I have to talk to you about this because it is having a knock-on effect on both department performance and customer service."

Discuss: "What is the problem, how can I help?"

Behaviour

Tell: "John, whenever I try to give you some feedback on your performance you get argumentative and defensive, it happened...... " (Facts from Aide memoir list)

Sell: "My job is to give feedback on performance when needed, it is what all managers have to do"

Discuss: "What do I need to do differently in the way I give you feedback that will not result in you getting emotional?"

Attendance

Tell: "Paul, you were late this morning what was the problem?"
"But you have been late 5 times in the past month." (Facts from Aide memoir list)

Sell: "You are contracted to start at 09:00 every morning and it would not be fair on the other team members if I allowed you to come into work late so often."

Discuss: "What is the problem?"

Step 4 – Sit down and discuss the big issues

It is now time to take a deep breath and grasp the nettle. Use the following structure for discussions:

Tell – Don't soft pedal; come straight out with your concerns, but do it in a polite, non-aggressive way.

Sell – Explain why you have to talk to them, how their behaviour/performance is affecting the business, and what improvement(s) are required.

Discuss – the situation and <u>confirm that what you are saying is correct.</u>

Agree – a plan of action for improvement, and offer what is needed to help them achieve the plan.

Motivate – try to leave them on a high by citing the plus points from the ☺side of the aide-memoire sheet. Remember this meeting is informal, so do not threaten them with their job; just holding the discussion will be perceived as a threat in itself.

Useful Tip:

Difficult people are <u>predictable</u> – it is their Achilles heel. If you know your people, you can easily predict what they are going to say, and how they are going to react – so prepare for it!

Issues and Actions

Planning

'The formulation of plans and actions to ensure the achievement of an objective'

Issues and Actions List

Issue – Deadlines and Documentation Accuracy

Actions:
- Contact supervisor before deadline time if there is a concern about a timescale
- Re-training on all documentation completion procedures by end of month
- Double check all information before submitting

Issue – Negative response to feedback on performance

Actions:
- Manager to give warning of feedback meeting to give time to prepare
- Review each feedback session on completion to ensure clarity of actions and effectiveness of discussion

Issue – Time-Keeping and Attendance

Actions:
- On all occassions contact office if going to be late
- When late, report to manager on arrival
- Attend 'Return to Work' interview on all instances of absence

Step 5 – Put together an agreed action plan

The Issues and Actions list:

An 'issues and actions list' is simply a 'to-do' list (actions) relating to the area requiring improvement (Issue).

Performance issues: The actions agreed should include training and coaching support. If the person has achieved the required standard previously, it should be made clear that this is retraining. It is **essential** that review dates should be included in the plan.

Behaviour issues: Apart from 'stop it', it is more difficult to put together some relevant improvement actions, so just saying "stop doing that" may be all you can do. It is essential though that you say "I will be monitoring the situation and giving you feedback (good/not-so-good) regularly."

Important point:

It is fair and reasonable for an employee to be <u>given time</u> to improve their performance, but employers have the right to ask for <u>immediate improvement</u> in poor behaviour.

See Example: Issues and Actions List – Appendix 17

Culture v Subculture

Subculture Influencer

'A function head/line manager within a large culture who possesses beliefs or interests at variance with those of the organisation'

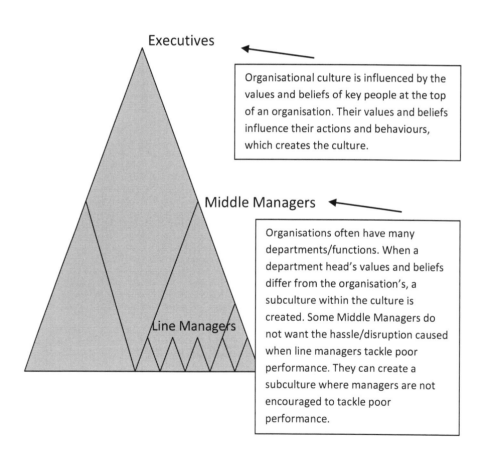

Executives

Organisational culture is influenced by the values and beliefs of key people at the top of an organisation. Their values and beliefs influence their actions and behaviours, which creates the culture.

Middle Managers

Organisations often have many departments/functions. When a department head's values and beliefs differ from the organisation's, a subculture within the culture is created. Some Middle Managers do not want the hassle/disruption caused when line managers tackle poor performance. They can create a subculture where managers are not encouraged to tackle poor performance.

Line Managers

Step 6 – Inform others of what you have done

Keep your bosses in the loop

Some organisations have a culture where poor performance is accepted rather than good performance being expected. The million dollar question is – will your company support you in what you have done? Unfortunately there are many Executives/middle managers who – because of fear (tribunals) – discourage the addressing of poor performance issues. It is imperative that you find out where you stand if you need to move the matter to more formal discussions (Disciplinary). The way to find this out is to let your boss know the facts, the damage it is causing to the business, and what you have done so far. You will know immediately if your boss is on your side by what they say and how they say it.

In larger organisations it is useful that you keep the HR team in the loop with what you have done, get them on board with what you are doing and together you can influence Executives' decisions.

Checking out the culture:

If you have a boss who will not support you in the addressing of poor performance, you have three options: 1. Go with the flow, 2. Rock the boat, 3. Find another boat.

The Paper Trail

Due Diligence
'To do something to protect yourself from blame or criticism'

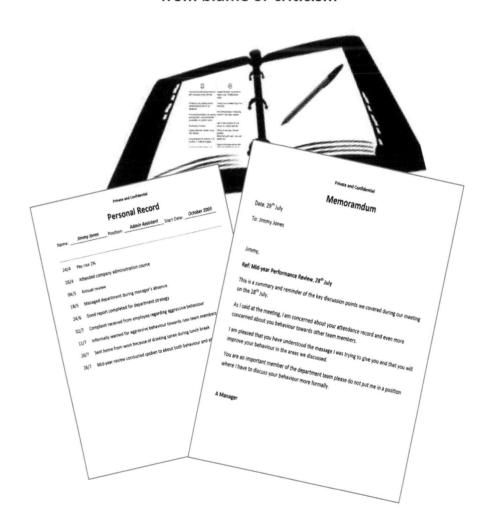

Step 7 – **N**otate everything!

You have now started a process where a certain amount of 'due diligence' is required because, if this person's performance does not improve (and you have to address the matter more formally) every fact, every note, and every document will become valuable components of the Paper trail.

The key documents you need to use are:–

Aide-memoire – This is a must!! Note down brief details of meeting (day, date and what was agreed) and continue to record facts as they happen. You may need to use the aide-memoire to write up a report if requested to.

Personnel Record – For more serious issues (normally poor behaviour) it may be wise to record a 'note on file'. This is a brief note listing day, date and what was agreed. If you make a note on someone's personnel file, the employee must be informed of this action.

Follow up letter - Very useful if you feel you have 'not got their attention'. A brief follow up letter is not only impactful but excellent 'due diligence'. The follow up letter should <u>not</u> be entitled 'Letter of Concern', this is too formal at this stage.

See Example: Note on File – Appendix 18

Fallout

'An adverse and unwanted side effect following a certain action'

Every Action has a Reaction

External fallout

Phone calls or unannounced visits from mothers, fathers, sisters, brothers and boyfriends, accusing you of bullying harassment.

Suggested response:

"Sorry but I'm not prepared to discuss the matter with you if XXXXXX is unhappy with what I said, he/she can always instigate the company grievance procedures"

Downward fallouts

Some disgruntled employees will go running to your boss or the HR department if you have one. If you have made your boss/HR Executive aware of the situation prior to discussion, there should be little to worry about. However some bosses may criticise your handling of the situation stating "you must've handle it wrong because the employee would not complain if you did it right."

Suggested response:

Show the Boss the facts, explain the damage that is being caused to the business and asked for their advice as to how to handle the situation.

If that fails say to your boss "I may not have the situation entirely right but what I was trying to do was right."

Step 8 – **G**et ready for some fallout

It does not matter how effective you are at communicating; some employees will see feedback as a reprimand (especially if they do not like you, or they have been 'getting away with it' for a while). At this stage, fallout tends to be slight, but you do need to monitor the person and be prepared for some repercussions.

Internal fallout:

▪ **'Bad mouth you' behind your back**
Not a real problem because your 'good' team members will applaud you – any other 'not so good' employees you may have will be worried that they are next on your list to be spoken to.

▪ **Quiet and subdued manner**
Re-motivate – give them something important to do, to make them feel important again. Let them know that the situation is 'water under the bridge'.

▪ **Telling others 'looking for another job'**
Keep the focus on their performance – by doing so you may actually 'persuade' them to find another job.

Note
Grievances, stress claims and constructive dismissal claims are covered in Chapter 10.

Chapter 8

The Formal process – Everybody has rights

Disciplinary Procedures

'The steps taken by an employer to correct serious performance or behaviour issues'

The Formal process – Everybody has rights

- Informal Actions and Procedures

- Semi-Formal Actions and Procedures

- First Stage Formal Actions and Procedures

- Second Stage Formal Actions and Procedures

- Final Stage Formal Actions and Procedures

- Gross Misconduct Actions and Procedures

- Appeal Procedures

Informal Actions and Procedures

Definition of Poor Performance

'When an employee's **performance** or **behaviour** falls below the required standard'

Step 1: Gather the Facts

- Line manager to notate (supervisory notes) instances of poor performance/behaviour
- Analysing and using the facts, identify the main areas of performance/ behaviour shortfall[1]

Step 2: Performance Review 1

- Line manager to conduct **one-to-one** meeting with employee to:
  - Discuss performance/behaviour concerns
- Formulate a **Personal Development Plan** outlining improvement actions and training and development requirements[2]
  - Express importance of achieving the required standards of performance/ behaviour within the required timescales
  - Potential consequences if standards are not achieved (**Performance Improvement Plan**)

Line Manager's rights:

- To expect employees to do what they are paid to do (**job description**) and behave appropriately whilst in the workplace (**company values**)

Poor Performance examples

- Poor work rate, productivity, financial targets
- Mistakes and errors
- Poor results, Incompletion of work, Missed deadlines

Poor behaviour examples

- Punctuality and Attendance
- Insubordination
- Laziness; Uncooperative, argumentative behaviour

Line Manager's rights:

- To talk to an employee when poor performance/behaviour is apparent
- Ask employees to perform/ behave to the required standard
- Set action plans and time scales for improved performance/ behaviour
- Take appropriate action if improvement is not achieved

Employee's rights:

- Evidence of poor performance
- Other employees treated in the same way
- Spoken to courteously and respectfully
- Appropriate training and coaching to achieve standard
- Adequate time to improve

Informal Actions and Procedures

Step 3: Employee and manager carry out agreed actions

- Employee works towards agreed actions plan (self-driven)
- Line manager to ensure training and support is provided as per PDP[3]
- Line manager to review progress on a regular basis, giving additional support when necessary

Line Manager's rights:

- To see effort being made to achieve the required standard
- Move to more formal discussions if employee makes insufficient effort in achieving the required standards

Step 4: Performance Review 2

- Line manager to conduct one-to-one meeting with employee to:
  - Discuss PDP progress
  - Assess if standards are being met
  - Assess effort being made
  - Decide the way forward if insufficient improvement is being achieved

Employee's rights:

- Evidence of continued poor performance
- Fair and objective assessment of progress and achievements
- Recognition of effort made
- Additional time to improve if progress is being made

[1] Everybody makes mistakes, misses deadlines and occasionally behaves inappropriately which can be resolved with a quiet word. Only persistent, consistent and important or sufficiently serious breaches in standards should be focused on

[2] Note of discussions and agreed actions to be recorded on employees' personal file

[3] Record to be made on **PDP** of all training, coaching and support given to employee

Line Manager's rights:

- Move to more formal discussions if employee has made insufficient effort to achieve the required standards
- Move to more formal discussions if the required standards are not achieved

Insufficient Improvement – more semi-formal procedures

Semi-Formal Actions and Procedures

Poor Performance continues despite time, training and support being given

Step 5: Employee is issued an Informal Performance Improvement Plan

- Line manager to conduct a further **one-to-one** meeting with employee to:
  - Discuss continued performance/ behaviour concerns
  - Identify any mitigating circumstances
  - Issue a **Performance Improvement Plan (PIP)** which outlines objectives, actions and timescales required[1]
  - Inform employee that progress and achievements will be reviewed on a regular basis giving additional support if employee struggles to achieve plan
  - Notify employee that failure to achieve the required standard may result in formal procedures being invoked
  - Confirm details of the meeting with a 'PIP confirmation letter'

Step 6: Employee implements Performance Improvement Plan

- Employee works towards the plan (self-driven)
- Line manager to ensure training and support is provided as per plan[3]
- Line manager to review progress on a regular basis giving additional support when needed if employee struggles to achieve plan[4]

Employee's rights:

- Evidence of continued poor performance
- Other employees treated in the same way and going through the same process[2]
- Spoken to courteously and respectfully
- Appropriate training and coaching provided
- Motivation and encouragement to achieve the requirements of the plan

Line Manager's rights:

- To take more formal action if plan is not adhered to, insufficient effort is observed, or the required improvement is not achieved

Employee's rights:

- Appropriate training and coaching
- The right amount of time to achieve the standards required
- Support and encouragement whilst working to the plan

Line Manager's rights:

- To move to more formal discussions <u>at any time</u> if employee makes insufficient effort or fails to work to plan

110

Semi-Formal Actions and Procedures continued

Step 7: Review of Performance **Improvement Plan**

- Line manager to conduct one-to-one$^{(5)}$ meeting with employee to:
  - Discuss PIP progress and achievements
  - Review progress being made
  - Assess effort being put into achieving the Performance Improvement Plan
  - Decide the way forward if insufficient improvement or effort is identified$^{(6)}$

Line Manager's rights:

- To take formal action if employee fails to make the required effort or the required standards of performance/behaviour are not being met

Employee's rights:

- Evidence of continued poor performance
- Fair and objective assessment of progress and achievements
- Additional time to improve if progress is being made $^{(6)}$

$^{(1)}$ Note on employee's personal file

$^{(2)}$ Critically important that other poor performing employees are treated accordingly

$^{(3)}$ Record made of all training and support provided to employee on training plan

$^{(4)}$ Results of progress reviews to be recorded

$^{(5)}$ This stage is still informal: a one-to-one discussions is still acceptable

$^{(6)}$ Sometimes advisable to extend timescale as moving into formal procedures should be a last resort

Insufficient Improvement – move to First Stage of the formal procedures

First Stage Formal Actions and Procedures

Poor Performance continues despite working to the plan and training and support being given

Employee's rights:
- Written notification or reasons for action
- Time to prepare for the meeting
- To be accompanied at the meeting
- Call witnesses if necessary

Step 8: Employee is instructed to attend a formal meeting:
- Line manager to conduct a further **one-to-one** meeting with employee to inform the employee that a formal discussion is to take place for: *'Failure to achieve the required standards of performance as outlined in the Performance Improvement Plan'* [1]
- Line manager to communicate to employee their rights in the matter

Employee's rights:
- Time to prepare
- To be accompanied
- Put their point of view across
- To present mitigating circumstances
- Call witnesses if appropriate
- To have a fair and objective (non-personal) hearing
- To not feel a decision had already been made re: sanction prior to the meeting being held

Step 9: Disciplinary Meeting 1
- Line manager to conduct disciplinary meeting:
  - Present the facts using the PIP as the focus of discussions [2]
  - Discuss mitigating circumstances
  - Call witnesses where appropriate

Employee's rights:
- Not have to wait too long for a decision to be made
- Previous achievements/ employment record to be taken into account
- Written notification as to action being taken
- The right of appeal
- Length of time sanction will be on record
- To be informed of possible consequences if performance does not improve

First Stage Formal Actions and Procedures continued

Step 10: Reconvene meeting

- Line manager to:
  - Communicate the sanction to be given[3]
  - Details on how long sanction is to last
  - Inform employee of company appeal procedures
  - Inform employee that the informal PIP will be upgraded to a formal PIP[4]
  - Record details in the employee's personnel record[5]

Employee's rights:

- Appropriate training and coaching
- Support and encouragement in achieving plan
- Extended time scales if objectives are not met but sufficient progress is being achieved

Line Manager's rights:

- To take formal action again if employee fails to make the required effort or the required standards of performance/ behaviour are not being met

[1] Keep reason for formal discussions clear and specific

[2] PIP to be used as both content and structure of meeting (seek advice first)

[3] Options: No formal warning but PIP to be extended, 1st written warning, or final warning if situation is sufficiently serious

[4] PIP to remain in place but formalised (re-titled Formal)

Insufficient Improvement – move to Second Stage of formal procedures

Second Stage Formal Actions and Procedures

This Stage is Optional – For smaller businesses (where appropriate) move to Final Stage

Poor Performance continues despite a formal warning having been given

Employee's rights:
- Evidence of continued poor performance
- Fair and objective assessment of progress and achievements
- Additional time to improve if progress is being made

Step 11: Review of Formal Performance Improvement Plan as per dates agreed
- Line manager to conduct one-to-one meeting with employee to:
  - Discuss formal PIP progress and achievements
  - Assess effort being put into achieving the performance plan
  - Decide the way forward if insufficient improvement or effort is identified

Line Manager's rights:
- To take further formal action if employee fails to make the required effort or the required standards of performance/behaviour are not being met

Step 12: Employee is instructed to attend a further disciplinary meeting for: *'Continued failure to achieve the required standards of performance as outlined in the Performance Improvement Plan'*

Employee's rights:
- Written notification or reasons for action
- Time to prepare for the meeting
- To be accompanied at the meeting
- To discuss mitigating circumstances
- Call witnesses where necessary

Second Stage Formal Actions and Procedures continued

Step 13: Disciplinary Meeting 2

- Line manager to conduct disciplinary meeting:
  - Present the facts
  - Discuss mitigating circumstances
  - Call witnesses where appropriate

Employee's rights:

- To be accompanied
- Put their point of view across to present mitigating circumstances
- Call witness if appropriate
- To have a fair and objective (non-personal) hearing
- To not feel a decision had already been made re: sanction achieved

Step 14: Adjourn

- Line manager to review facts
- Take mitigating circumstances into consideration
- Discuss facts and recommendations with senior managers or support services (HR) if needed

Employee's rights:

- Written notification as to action being taken
- The right of appeal
- Length of time sanction will be on record
- To be informed of possible consequences if performance does not improve

Step 15: Reconvene meeting

- Line manager to:
  - Communicate the sanction to be given
  - Details on how long sanction is to last, generally not longer than one year
  - Inform employee of company appeal procedures
  - Inform employee that the formal PIP will be reviewed and re-issued
  - Employee notified that failure to achieve the required standard may result in further disciplinary action being taken, which *may* include Dismissal with notice

Employee's rights:

- Written notification as to action being taken
- The right of appeal
- Length of time sanction will be on record
- To be informed of possible consequences if performance does not improve

Insufficient Improvement – move to Final Stage of formal procedures

Final Stage Formal Actions and Procedures

Poor Performance continues despite a Final warning having been issued

Employee's rights:
- Evidence of no improvement or insufficient improvement in poor performance
- Fair and objective assessment of progress and achievements

Step 16: Review of Formal Performance Improvement Plan as per dates agreed
- Line manager to conduct one-to-one [5] meeting with employee to:
  - Discuss formal PIP progress and achievements
  - Assess effort being put into achieving the performance plan
  - Decide the way forward if insufficient improvement or effort is identified

Line Manager's rights:
- To Dismiss if employee has failed to make the required effort or the required standards of performance/ behaviour are not being met

Step 17: Employee is instructed to attend a further disciplinary meeting for:

'Continued failure to achieve the required standards of performance as outlined in the Performance Improvement Plan'

Employee's rights:
- Written notification or reasons for action
- **To be informed that meeting may result in dismissal**
- Time to prepare for the meeting
- To be accompanied at the meeting
- To discuss mitigating circumstances
- Call witnesses where necessary

[5] All details to be recorded in employee's personal record

Final Stage Formal Actions and Procedures

Step 18: Disciplinary Meeting 2

- Senior Manager to conduct disciplinary meeting:
  - Present the facts
  - Discuss mitigating circumstances
  - Call witnesses where appropriate

Employee's rights:
- To be accompanied
- To put their point of view across
- To present mitigating circumstances
- Call witness if appropriate
- To have a fair and objective (non-personal) hearing
- To not feel a decision had already been made re: sanction

Step 19: Adjourn

- Senior Manager to review facts
- Take mitigating circumstances into consideration
- Discuss facts and recommendations with line managers or support services (HR) if needed

Step 20: Reconvene meeting

- Senior Manager to:
- Dismiss employee or extend Final notice period
- Inform employee of appeals procedure
- Explain termination of employment payment details

Employee's rights:
- Written notification as to why action was taken
- The right of appeal

Gross Misconduct Actions & Procedures

Gross Misconduct

An employee acts in such a way that justifies possible dismissal

Examples (Not exhaustive):
- Theft or Fraud
- Physical violence or bullying
- Internet abuse
- Serious act of insubordination
- Incapacity of work through drink or drugs
- Serious breach of H&S
- Deliberate damage to company equipment

Step 1: Investigate incident
- Line manager appoints a colleague or senior manager to conduct an investigation [1]
- Investigating manager gathers the facts and presents facts to the line manager with recommendations
- Line manager decides if formal discussions need to take place

Employee's rights:
- To be accompanied during fact finding discussions. Although not a 'right' by law it is advisable

When formal discussions are necessary line manager to inform employee of the decision that a disciplinary meeting is to take place

Employee's rights:
- The reason for the meeting (in writing)
- Possible consequences
- Adequate time to prepare
- To be accompanied during the meeting

Step 2: Line manager conducts disciplinary meeting
- Presents and discusses facts with employee
- Discuss mitigating circumstances
- Call witnesses where appropriate

Employee's rights:
- To be accompanied during the meeting
- To be able to present their views on the facts
- To present mitigating circumstances
- Call witness if appropriate

Gross Misconduct Actions & Procedures continued

Step 3: Manager adjourns to make a decision

- Line manager review facts and discussions
- Take mitigating circumstances into consideration
- Where necessary, discuss facts and recommendations with senior managers or support services (HR)
- Decide appropriate level of sanction

Employee's rights:
- To have their general record of behaviour/performance taken into consideration before a sanction is decided

Step 4: Reconvene meeting

- Line manager to communicate sanction to be given and why it is necessary
- Inform employee of company appeal procedures

Employee's rights:
- To be informed in writing of sanction being imposed
- Reason for action being taken
- The right of appeal

Dismissal – (Normal for gross misconduct issues)
- Employee leaves the organisation immediately

Final written warning or demotion (in exceptional circumstances) (2)

(1) Judgment call, as it is appropriate that an employee's line manager conducts all formal discussions

(2) In exceptional circumstances (violence, threatening behaviour) a final written warning rather than dismissal may be issued

119

Appeal

'A process for requesting a formal change to an official decision'

Appeal Procedures

It is every employee's right to appeal against a formal decision

Appeals Procedure

The Normal Procedures

- The employee has up to seven days to submit an appeal following receipt of formal letter
- The appeal should be addressed to a senior manager other than the manager who issued the warning
- The appeal letter should clearly outline the basis for the appeal
- Senior manager or company representative should hear the appeal within 7 days of receipt of appeal letter

Employee's rights:

- To appeal if they feel the action taken is wrong, or unjust
- To have the appeal heard by someone different to the person who issued the sanction
- The hearing to be conducted in a fair and reasonable way
- Time to prepare for the appeal meeting
- To call witnesses where appropriate
- To be accompanied at the hearing
- To be informed of the next stages if the appeal is not upheld

Employer's rights:

- The basis for the appeal to be clearly outlined.
- To increase the severity of the sanction if merited

Chapter 9

Every Action has a Reaction

Reaction
**'The way someone acts or feels in response
to something that happens or is said'**

Chapter 9 – Every Action has a Reaction

- Organisational Politics
- Bullying and Harassment Accusations
- Abuse of Power
- You are picking on me because I am ……….
- The Stress Card
- The Constructive Dismissal Claim

Organisational Politics

It's hard to think you could get into a political situation just by asking someone to behave or perform to the required standard, but it does happen. Other people in your organisation may have their own agendas and self-interests, so it's important that you are aware of this in order for you to manage the situation, if it arises.

Politics with the boss – What if your boss once managed or even recruited this employee? What if this employee has a long-term personal relationship with your boss? If this is the case, you could get into an uncomfortable relationship with your boss. If there is a possibility of this go to your boss, explain the problem/the damage being caused, and ask for their advice as to what to do.

Your boss and the support functions (HR) – You could also be caught up in a political situation between your boss and the HR function. This is often caused by your manager wanting to do X and the HR advisers suggesting you do Y. At the end of the day you have to do <u>what your boss wants you to do</u>. If HR do not agree with a certain course of action then that is between them, and it should not involve you. However, you may be seen as causing the problem.

Political manoeuvring from your colleagues – You may experience some political manoeuvring from your peers/ colleagues also as they may have managed this employee before and not done anything about it, and because you are exposing their reluctance to tackle poor performance. You can certainly get into a political situation but 'forewarned is forearmed.'

Organisational Politics
'The pursuit of individual agendas and self-interests with little regard to the effect on the organisation's efforts to achieve its goals'

Bullying and Harassment Accusations

Many accusations of bullying and harassment result from discussions about poor performance: employees make this accusation because it is an easy thing to do. It is a 'don't mess with me' message and a method of getting you to back off. Some employees also think that doing this will discredit you in the eyes of your bosses. Knowing the key differences between bullying and harassment and being aware of the behaviours associated with each, is key to defending this accusation.

Bullying – If the employee is accusing you of bullying this means they are accusing you of:

- Yelling or screaming
- Using inappropriate language, i.e. Swearing
- Angry outbursts directed at them
- Aggressive posture or invading their personal space
- Using aggressive hand gestures
- Undermining them behind their back
- Ridiculing – making them look stupid
- Name calling
- Inappropriate comments on personal appearance
- Malicious teasing
- Playing pranks and practical jokes
- Negative comments in front of others

Management style

Some of the previously mentioned behaviours can be seen as bullying when they are actually management 'style'. If you have <u>not</u> behaved in any of the previously mentioned (page 126) ways, the employee will have a real problem accusing you of bullying.

See Bullying and Harassment Behaviours summary – Appendix 19

Bullying
'Deliberate negative behaviour being aimed at an individual (or individuals), repeatedly and persistently over time'

Harassment – is normally linked to some type of discrimination and there are clear laws against this. If you were being accused of **harassment,** this means you have been focusing your attention on them because of their:

- Sexuality
- Disability
- Age
- Race or Religion
- Sexual orientation
- Gender re-assignment

If you do not want to be accused of this, do not:

- Make offensive remarks
- Make innuendos
- Make unfair comments
- Have unnecessary one-on-ones
- Use subjective words
- Have any personal contact
- Invade an employee's personal space

The Legal Tenet (Principle) of Harassment or Bullying is:
'Would a reasonable person observing this behaviour/action(s) view this as harassment or bullying?' This means, if it looks like harassment and/or bullying, it probably is.

If you have <u>not</u> behaved in any of the previously mentioned (page 128) ways the employee will have a real problem accusing you of Harassment.

See Bullying and Harassment Behaviours summary – Appendix 19

Harassment

'Uninvited, unwanted, unwarranted attention that affects someone's dignity in the workplace'

Abuse of Power

Abuse of Power and Authority

There can also be accusations of bullying by the **Abuse of Power**, which is when a manager deliberately uses their authority to bully and intimidate employees who do not conform, or who challenge them. This definitely does happen: it is very easy for a manager to 'make life difficult' for someone if they want to. If you do not want to be accused of this, do not deliberately:

- Give excessive and harsh criticism of work performance
- Isolate employees from each other by delegating tasks aimed at keeping them apart
- Ignore the employee
- Hold back productive work
- Distribute workload unfairly
- Request unnecessary work to be done
- Set unachievable deadlines
- Set unachievable tasks and objectives
- Undermine work performance
- Devalue work effort
- Fail to give credit where credit is due

If you have not done any of the above actions, the employee will have a real problem accusing you of abusing your power as the manager.

See Bullying and Harassment Behaviours summary – Appendix 19

Abuse of Power
'Improper use of authority by using one's position to manipulate in an abusive way'

"You are picking on me because I am............"
Accusation

Discrimination accusation

You will one day be having a difficult conversation with an employee and the employee will accuse you of picking on them because they are: black, old, female/male, gay etc. It happens when the employee feels that they are under attack, and it is made to spook you and get you to back off. DO NOT BE SPOOKED by this comment. You can use what was said to your advantage if you respond to it correctly. When this comment is made:

- Coolly reach for a pen and paper
- Holding the pen in the writing position ask the employee to 'repeat what they just said' and write it down. Make them repeat it!
- Pause and then say, "Give me an example of where I have treated you any differently from the other people in the team?"
- Do not let him/her off the hook: keep asking the same question until you get either an apology for making the remark or the usual
  "I cannot think of anything at the moment" response.
- When you get either of those two replies, say the following:

"When you made that comment, you made a serious accusation of discrimination. What I <u>have</u> to do now is report your accusation to the company, and you will be written to regarding the organisation's policy on discrimination and the procedures you must take if you feel you are being discriminated against. I will (of course) also be reporting the fact that you were unable to substantiate that accusation".

Important note - When you ask the "give me an example" question, you must listen carefully because if this person genuinely feels that you <u>are</u> discriminating, then you have to listen to each instance and give an explanation or apology if the instance did actually happen and was unintentional.

Discrimination
'The unjust treatment of different categories of people, especially on the grounds of race, age or sex'

The Stress Card

There are numerous ways in which workplace stress can be caused. Two big stress causes are: 1. unclear roles and responsibilities and 2. lack of support and direction from above. The big problem to managers here is that when you give a poorly performing employee clarity with regards to their role, and try to give them some direction and support, they go off work sick with stress! It really is a catch twenty-two situation. It is a fact that **many stress claims result from discussions of poor performance.** The manager gives constructive feedback on performance, the employee does not like what is being said and the next day they call in sick with stress as the cause. There are a number of things that may help you manage this situation:

Speak to Boss/HR

If there is even a hint that this person is likely to go off sick with stress, speak to your boss or HR before speaking to them. Explain the situation, the damage to the team/business by their poor performance and get their SUPPORT and ADVICE. Sometimes it is better that you hold back from a difficult discussion while you get people/things in place before the discussion. If an employee is reporting stress, expect a long period away from work.

Long-term sickness – can be defined as 'away from work for a period of 20 days or more'. This means the employee's attendance becomes a company issue rather than just yours. When the company is involved they can instruct Occupational Health Doctors, home visits etc.

Do not fear stress claims – they are exceptionally difficult to prove. The employee will have to prove that you breached your duty of care, the working environment posed a real risk to their health, and that it was foreseeable by you/the organisation. Very difficult to prove if this was not the case.

Stress
'The adverse effect on health caused by excessive pressures or demands placed on employees at work'

The Constructive Dismissal Claim

Constructive dismissal is a form of dismissal. When an employee is forced to resign from their job because of their employer's conduct, they can pursue a claim for unfair dismissal. To do this, the employer must have committed a serious breach of contract and the employee must give evidence of it. Examples may include:

- A serious breach of the employee's contract (e.g. not paying them or suddenly demoting them for no reason)
- Forcing the employee to accept unreasonable changes to their conditions of employment without their agreement (e.g. suddenly telling them to work in another town, or making them work night shifts when they are contracted for day work only)
- Bullying, harassment or violence against them by colleagues
- Making the employee work in dangerous conditions

Constructive dismissal claims are very difficult to prove and very few go to a full tribunal because very rarely is there a fundamental breach of the employee's contract.

If an employee or an employee's representative instigates a constructive dismissal claim, DON'T be spooked because if you have clear facts and a paper trail there is little to worry about.

Constructive Dismissal
'When an employee is forced to terminate the contract under which he/she is employed because of the employer's conduct'

Chapter 10

Grievance Procedures – <u>Everybody</u> has rights

Grievance
'A real or imagined wrong or other
cause for complaint or protest'

Grievance Procedures – <u>Everybody</u> has rights

- Grievance 1 – Terms and Conditions
- Grievance 2 – Co-worker
- Grievance 3 – Line Manager
- Appeal procedures
- Investigating Grievances

Grievance 1 – Terms and Conditions

Grievance Procedures 1

Employee grievance relating to terms and conditions or working practices

Step 1: Informal Notification to line manager (Verbal)

- Employee verbally informs line manager of their complaint
- Employee gives manager reasonable time to respond and resolve the matter

Employee is dissatisfied with line manager's response to complaint: Proceed to Step 2

Line Manager's responsibilities:

- To take responsibility for resolving grievance (not to pass it on to others)
- To treat the complaint seriously, objectively, and independently
- To not respond without considering matter carefully
- To respond to the employee's complaint within a reasonable time
- To take the matter to the senior management and discuss possible outcomes
- To arrange a meeting and give employee an opportunity to discuss the matter
- To communicate to the employee the company decision/position on the matter.

Employee's rights:

- Matter to be looked at quickly
- To be kept confidential where appropriate
- A clear response regarding grievance
- An appeal process if not satisfied with response.

Grievance 1 – Terms and Conditions continued

Step 2: Formal notification of grievance to line manager (Written)

- Employee to write to line manager stating why dissatisfied with response and to formally lodge a grievance setting out the grounds of complaint
- Employee gives manager reasonable time to arrange more formal discussions

Employee is dissatisfied with line manager's response to complaint: Proceed to Step 3

Step 3: Appeal

- Employee to write to senior manager stating why dissatisfied with response and to formally lodge an appeal
- Employee gives senior manager reasonable time to investigate and arrange appeal meeting

Employee's rights:

- To be accompanied at the meeting[1]
- To be given the opportunity of discussing the matter more formally with line manager/company representative
- To be listened to objectively and fairly
- A reasonable explanation as to why the decision was made
- Outcomes of the meeting[2] communicated in writing

Senior Manager's responsibilities:

- To respond to the employee's appeal within a reasonable time
- To investigate issues and make a final decision re the outcome
- To arrange mediation if necessary [3]

---

[1] Grievance meeting may sometimes be held by a company representative with a manager attending

[2] Notes will be taken during the meeting

[3] Mediation is only an option if it is part of the company's terms and conditions of employment

Grievance 2 – Co-worker

Grievance Procedures 2

Employee's complaint relating to a co-worker's conduct or behaviour

Step 1: Informal discussion with line manager (Verbal)

- Employee verbally informs line manager of their grievance and the facts of the matter
- Employee must give line manager reasonable time to investigate and try to resolve complaint informally

Employee is dissatisfied with line manager's management of complaint move to Step 2:

(1) Every manager has a duty to provide a safe working environment for their staff. Grievances/complaints taken out by employees about other employees can and should be resolved by the line manager using informal/formal procedures professionally

(2) Due diligence step: it is advisable for the line manager to inform more senior manager/HR adviser of the complaint

(3) All complaints must be treated seriously as not resolving them could result in a grievance being taken out against the line manager for mismanagement of the matter

Line Manager's responsibilities:

- Treat the complaint seriously[1]
- Inform senior management of the complaint [2]
- To confidentially and tactfully monitor the situation in order to confirm complaint is valid[3]
- To help/advise the employee in resolving the matter themselves
- Invoke company informal/formal procedures if inappropriate behaviour is observed.

Employee's rights:

- To have the matter treated confidentially , objectively and tactfully without aggravating the situation
- To see the line manager actively monitoring the situation
- To see the line manager addressing any instance of inappropriate behaviour using the company formal/informal procedures
- To take a formal grievance out against the line manager if the matter is mismanaged in any way

Grievance 2 – Co-worker continued

Step 2: Formal notification of grievance against their line manager (Written)

- Employee to write to senior manager stating why they are dissatisfied with the way their complaint is being managed
- Employee gives senior management reasonable time to investigate matter and arrange more formal discussions

Senior Manager's responsibilities:

- To investigate thoroughly the manager's handling of the situation
- To respond to the employee's grievance within a reasonable time
- To arrange a meeting and give employee an opportunity to present their case [4]
- To instruct the line manager in the way the matter should be handled if being handled incorrectly

Employee is dissatisfied with Company's response to grievance:

Step 3: Appeal

- Employee to write to senior manager stating why dissatisfied with response and to formally lodge an appeal
- Employee gives senior manager reasonable time to investigate and arrange appeal meeting.

Employee's rights:

- To be accompanied at the meeting
- To be given the opportunity of discussing the matter more formally with line manager/ company representative
- To be listened to objectively and fairly
- A reasonable explanation as to why the issue is not being addressed
- Outcomes of the meeting communicated in writing without unreasonable delay [5]

Senior Manager's responsibilities:

- To respond to the employee's appeal within a reasonable time
- To investigate issues and make a final decision re the outcome
- To take matter to mediation if this is part of the company procedures. [6]
- To be listened to objectively and fairly.

[4] Grievance meetings may sometimes be held by a company representative with a manager attending.
[5] Notes will be taken during the meeting.
[6] Mediation is only an option if it is part of the company terms and contracts of employment.

Grievance 3 – Line Manager

Grievance Procedures 3

Employee grievance relating to line manager's behaviour

Step 1: Formal notification of grievance to senior manager (Written)

- Employee to write to senior manager outlining their complaint, stating the facts & corroborating evidence.
- Employee gives senior management reasonable time to arrange fact finding meetings.

Step 2: Fact finding to be conducted involving all relevant parties

Line Manager's rights:

- To not be prejudged before the investigation is conducted
- To be made aware of the facts of the complaint before a fact-finding meeting is arranged with them [1]
- To attend a meeting in order to present their views on the facts and call witnesses where necessary
- To be accompanied at the meeting
- To be treated courteously and objectively during the fact-finding process

Senior Manager's responsibilities:

- Acknowledge that the complaint has been received
- Arrange and conduct a meeting with the employee to discuss the complaint and review facts
- Arrange and conduct a meeting with line manager to discuss the facts and the complaint made against them
- Investigate the matter fairly, objectively and timely
- Ensure neither party feels threatened or insecure during the fact-finding process, which may include suspending one or both from the workplace during the investigation process

Employee's rights:

- To have a meeting arranged in order to present the facts and call witnesses where necessary
- To be accompanied at the meeting
- To be treated courteously and objectively during the fact-finding process

[1] The employee has made a potential gross misconduct accusation against the line manager, it is only right that they can review the facts of the grievance and prepare for discussions.

Grievance 3 – Line Manager continued

Step 3: Senior manager reviews the facts and makes a decision as to the right course of action:

- Senior manager communicates decision to both employee and line manager.
  - If the complaint is not upheld the employee is informed as to the reasons and informed of the appeal process.
  - If the complaint is upheld the line manager is made aware of the reasons and informed of the appeal process.
  - If the complaint is upheld the employee is informed of this and made aware of the action that the company will be implementing to avoid a reoccurrence of the matter.

Senior Manager's responsibilities:
- To investigate thoroughly and objectively the manager's handling of the situation
- To arrange a meeting and give employee an opportunity to present their case
- To instruct the line manager in the way the matter should be handled if being handled incorrectly

Employee's rights:
- To appeal against the decision made and be accompanied
- To see appropriate action being taken if the grievance is upheld
- Outcome of the meeting communicated in writing without unreasonable delay

Employee or Line Manager is dissatisfied with Company's response to grievance:

Line Manager's rights:
- To appeal against the decision made and to be accompanied at the appeal
- To fair treatment if the complaint is upheld
- The right actions towards the employee if the complaint is deemed to have been spurious or vexatious [2]
- Outcomes of the meeting communicated in writing without unreasonable delay

Step 4: Appeal

- Employee or Line Manager to write to senior manager stating why dissatisfied with response and to formally lodge an appeal
- Employee gives senior manager reasonable time to investigate and arrange appeal meeting

[2] If the grievance is not upheld and proven to be:
  - **Spurious*** (false, bogus, forged)
  - **Vexatious** (Deliberate attempt to disparage, discredit, undermine, cause harm and discomfort)

corrective action needs to be taken with the employee (which may include disciplinary action or dismissal) and the line manager made aware of this action.

Spurious
**'Not being what it claims to be:
False, bogus, no basis of fact'**

Vexatious
**'Deliberate attempt to disparage, discredit,
undermine, cause harm and discomfort'**

Grievance 3 – Investigating Grievances

Investigating grievances that occurred as a result of discussions regarding poor performance.

1. Evidence:
– At the time of the discussion was there clear evidence of poor performance by the employee?
– What does the employee need to improve to bring them up to the required standard of performance?

2. Method:
– What methods were used by the line manager to address this employee's poor performance i.e. counselling, discussion, performance plan?
– Was the process used in-line with the company performance management procedures?
– Was the method used relevant to the seriousness of the performance issue?
– Is the manager addressing others in the team with similar performance issues?

3. Manner: (Communication style of line manager)
During discussions with the employee did the line manager at any time:
– Shout?
– Threaten – apart from explaining the consequences?
– Get angry or use threatening body language?
– Say or do anything unprofessional?
– Abuse their position as manager in any way?

Decision – Uphold or not Uphold Complaint

Summary

Integrity
'Doing the right things when nobody is watching'

Summary

- The WIIFM Factor
- Continuous Self Development

Self Esteem
'A feeling of pride or worthiness in oneself'

The WIIFM Factor

What's in it for me?

Tackling poor performance is certainly challenging, uncomfortable, time consuming and undoubtedly risky, so why bother? Why not just maintain the status quo, not make waves and do what many other managers do and aim for a quiet, easy, working environment? You must admit it is tempting, but there are a number of important benefits that will outweigh the negatives if you don't tolerate poor performance:

Money – Managers who are effective in managing poor performance deliver better results than other managers, because they do not have poor performers dragging down the team. Because of this they out-perform other managers, get bigger pay rises and earn bigger bonuses.

Respect and Credibility – Managers who tackle poor performance effectively are held in high esteem by their bosses and their team members. Managers who do not tackle poor performance lose respect and credibility, and expose their lack of integrity.

Career Advancement – If you are interested in moving up the corporate ladder, show your executives that you can tackle poor performance. It is one skill that many middle managers lack.

Your Job Security – If you do not tackle poor performance, it will come back and shoot you in the foot one day. Something will happen which will expose your reluctance and then <u>you</u> will be seen as a poor manager, and you will experience 'the performance management process'.

Self Esteem – You will never feel proud or worthy if you put up with poor performance or let poor performers walk all over you.

Continuous Self Development

Things to do to develop your skills

The More of, Less of, Differently Technique – Learn from every experience. Every time you tackle a performance issue review how you did by asking yourself the following question: *"If I knew then what I know now, what would I have done: more of, less of, or differently?"* Constantly do this and you will get a better result every time.

Train and Coach Someone – There is no better way of developing your poor performance management skills than training and coaching others when they have to do it. Become the Performance Management Coach and watch your credibility rise and your career prospects increase.

Learn and then Learn some more – Managers have an in-depth knowledge of their company's products and have a fair understanding of the job they are paid to do. Surprisingly though, few managers go out of their way to study, research and learn about the HR aspects of a manager's job, even though it is a big part of their role. You do not need to go on training courses, because the web is full of learning, if you know where to look for it. Try these sites, they are a great way of learning:–

www.hrzone.co.uk - No subscription and a great way of asking questions.

www.ACAS.org.uk – Not a great help in dealing with poor performance as the advice is either about Gross misconduct or is procedural information. However, it is worth looking at because it communicates changes in employment legislation in a language that is easy to understand. Once you are signed up, these sites will keep you updated with all changes in employment legislation.

See Your Personal Development Plan – Appendix 20

Continuous Self Development

'The process of committing oneself to improving knowledge and understanding throughout a career'

Courage

'The ability to do something that frightens you'

The Word Quiz

What is the word or phrase that relates to the definition/ statement? (All answers can be found somewhere in this book!!)

	Definition/Statement	Word or Phrase?
1	A word or phrase that is often repeated, which expresses a particular strong belief	
2	When an employee's performance <u>or</u> behaviour 'falls below the required standard' (Legal definition)	
3	Being in charge of someone and of making sure that what they are required to do is done satisfactorily or well	
4	To allow without prohibiting or opposing	
5	The quality of being believed or trusted	
6	Unwillingness or disinclination to do something necessary or important	
7	The area of Law that covers all aspects of employer and employee relationships	
8	Improving organisations and working life through better employment relations	
9	An Executive list, plan, outline of things to be achieved, in order to improve overall business performance	
10	Free from bias, dishonesty, or injustice and the standard of care that a reasonably prudent person would observe under a given set of circumstances	
11	A specific result that a person aims to achieve within a specific timeframe	
12	The practice of using tools, procedures and techniques to develop, correct or reward performance	

13	Confident and direct in claiming one's rights or putting one's views across	
14	A thing that is indisputably the case	
15	A clear and detailed written plan relating to the work that is to be performed or the behaviour that needs to change	
16	A brief record of facts written down to aid memory kept – together with information set down in writing – as a means of evidence	
17	The practice of carrying out less urgent tasks in preference to more urgent ones, thus putting off impending tasks to a later time	
18	The accomplishment of a given task measured against known standards of: accuracy, completeness, cost or speed	
19	A written agreement specifying terms and conditions under which an employee consents to perform, in return for an agreed wage or salary	
20	A process or period in which an employee's suitability is assessed and for an employee to assess the suitability of an organisation	
21	Principles, standards or qualities considered worthwhile or desirable to an organisation	
22	A powerful culture influencing tool, communicating expectations relating to conduct and behaviour within the workplace	
23	To be used following an informal meeting with an employee to highlight a concern when disciplinary action is not necessary	
24	A formal discussion to determine a suitable course of action	
25	The action of going to or being present at a place or event	
26	A process to influence a culture where regular attendance is expected rather than irregular attendance being accepted	

27	Gathered factual absence information for analysis, problem solving and action planning	
28	Instances of absence multiplied by total amount of days = S^2 Total number of days taken over a period= D. $S^2 \times D =$	
29	Actions and mannerisms displayed by people in conjunction with their environment	
30	The process by which a manager evaluates an employee's work performance and behaviour	
31	An opportunity for an employee to share concerns about their illness and general state of health in relation to their job	
32	A formal document to assist organisations in the management of Statutory Sickness	
33	Taking action immediately in order to deal with a difficult or unpleasant situation	
34	A pattern of letters that assists in remembering something important or significant	
35	The key link between informal and formal discussions	
36	To assess a situation with the intention of implementing necessary change	
37	An immediate, reflex reaction made without thought, analysis or planning	
38	Communicating progress and achievement information as a basis for improvement or recognition	
39	A function head/line manager within a large culture who possesses beliefs or interests at variance with those of the organisation	
40	To do something to protect yourself from blame or criticism	
41	An adverse and unwanted side effect following a certain action	
42	The steps taken by an employer to correct serious performance or behaviour issues	

43	A process for requesting a formal change to an official decision	
44	The way someone acts or feels in response to something that happens or is said	
45	Deliberate negative behaviour being aimed at an individual (or individuals) repeatedly and persistently over time	
46	Uninvited, unwanted, unwarranted attention that affects someone's dignity in the workplace	
47	Improper use of authority by using one's position to manipulate in an abusive way	
48	The unjust treatment of different categories of people, especially on the grounds of race, age or sex	
49	The adverse effect on health caused by excessive pressures or demands placed on employees at work	
50	When an employee is forced to terminate the contract under which he/she is employed for reason of the employer's conduct	
51	A real or imagined wrong or other cause for complaint or protest	
52	Not being what it claims to be: false, bogus, no basis in fact	
53	Deliberate attempt to disparage, discredit, undermine, cause harm and discomfort	
54	Doing the right things when nobody is watching	
55	A feeling of pride or worthiness in oneself	
56	The process of committing oneself to improving knowledge and understanding throughout a career	
57	The ability to do something that frightens you	
58	The feeling or belief that one can rely on oneself	
59	Steadfast in doing something despite the difficulties and challenges	
60	Conformity in the application of something necessary for the sake of fairness	

Your Score:

Important Note

Every word and definition in this quiz is important – managers should know them all.

Appendices

Appendix 1 – Cost: of Poor Performance

Appendix 2 – Fair and Reasonable Charter

Appendix 3 – Performance Management Tool Kit

Appendix 4 – Example: Aide Memoire list

Appendix 5 – Example: Performance Improvement Plan

Appendix 6 – Example: Objectives based Job Description

Appendix 7 – Example: Poor Performance Procedures

Appendix 8 – Example: Induction Objectives (Line Manager)

Appendix 9 – Example: Induction Objectives (Employee)

Appendix 10 – Example: Appraisal (Poor Performer)

Appendix 11 – Example: Company Values

Appendix 12 – Example: Personal Improvement Plan

Appendix 13 – Example: Letter of Concern

Appendix 14 – Example: Sickness Record

Appendix 15 – Full explanation of the Bradford Factor

Appendix 16 – Example: Self Certification Form

Appendix 17 – Example: Issues and Actions List

Appendix 18 – Example: Note on File

Appendix 19 – Bullying and Harassment Behaviours summary

Appendix 20 – Your Personal Development Plan

Appendix 1 – Cost of Poor Performance

Case Studies

Case Study 1: Sales Manager D tolerated poor performance within his sales team. He walked away from confrontation and was quite prepared to give up his 'employer rights' for the sake of peace and harmony. Because Manager D's organisation traded in a growth industry, Manager D's financial results were comparable with other Sales Managers within the organisation. However Executives within this organisation felt that sales achievements were being achieved '***despite** this manager rather than because of this manager's performance'*. After many years within the role, Manager D left the organisation to pursue another career path. The new Sales Manager was a competent manager who did not tolerate poor performance and, recognising the fact that he was 'inheriting' a poor sales team, immediately set about addressing poor performance. It took six months to 'improve or remove' poor performing sales team members and as a result sales increased by 23% above company average over the first full year of Manager E's appointment.

Case Study 2: Manager F was the Section Manager in a large accounts department; he had also tolerated poor performance within the team. Manager F had previously experienced a formal grievance and was now completely risk adverse as he feared a further grievance claim if he again tried to address the long term performance issues within the team. Financial statistics showed that operating costs in the section were always **circa 11% higher** than other comparable business Sections in the organisation. This increase in costs was caused by numerous attendance issues, high staff turnover and low productivity. When Manager F left the organisation Manager G was appointed and set about addressing the poor attendance issues and staff turnover. During the first full year of Manager G's appointment, operating costs fell in line with the other business units. This circa 11% reduction in operating costs equated to a net saving **in excess of £62k.** Manager F had held this management position for over **18 years.**

Case Study 3: In the Retail Industry, the warehouse is seen as the engine room of a retail unit. If the warehouse is under-performing, sales and customer service will always be badly affected. Peter was a poor performing Warehouse Manager: he was not an effective team leader, he tolerated poor performance within the warehouse team, and his organisational skills were in need of a great deal of development. Peter went on long-term sick leave because of stress caused by the demands of the Warehouse Manager role. An experienced Warehouse Manager was drafted in on a 'covering' basis. This covering warehouse manager immediately set about bringing the warehouse up to the required standards. As a consequence there was immediate improvement in the service within the retail unit and (within one month) the retail unit was achieving its sales targets, where before it had always struggled. After being away sick for six months Peter returned to work. Within a short period of time the warehouse operation again became disorganised and the retail unit again suffered service and sales issues. With analysis, it was confirmed that sales had increased by an average of **26%** during Peter's absence. When calculated over a year, this retail unit would have achieved in excess of **£200k** additional sales if Peter had not been the warehouse manager in place.

Appendices

Appendix 2 – Fair and Reasonable Charter

The Fair & Reasonable Charter

It is both Fair and Reasonable for employers to expect employees to:

- **Do the job they are paid to do (Performance)**
- **Behave appropriately while at work (Behaviour)**
- **Turn up for work when they are meant to (Attendance)**

When any of these expectations are not being met, Employers have a right to use Disciplinary and Dismissal procedures to resolve the problem if they have:

- Clear <u>evidence</u> of poor performance, behaviour or attendance.
- Made the Employee <u>aware</u> of the facts and the exact nature of their concerns.
- Made clear to the Employee the standard of performance or behaviour that is <u>expected</u>.
- Provided the Employee with appropriate <u>training or support</u> to help them to improve.
- Given the Employee <u>adequate time to improve</u>.
- Made clear to the Employee the <u>potential consequences</u> of failing to achieve the required standard of performance.
- Treated all Employees <u>in the same way</u>.
- <u>Written evidence</u> that all the points on the Charter have been followed.

Implementing the principles of this Charter will help Employers handle disciplinary and dismissal issues in a **Fair and Reasonable** way, a key requirement of Legislation today.

Appendix 3 – Performance Management Tool Kit

The Performance Management Tool Kit

Which of these tools do you use to help you manage employee performance?

	Never Used	Sometimes Used	Always Used
• Contracts of employment	☐	☐	☐
• Employee handbooks	☐	☐	☐
• Job descriptions	☐	☐	☐
• Key Performance Indicators (KPIs)	☐	☐	☐
• Probationary periods	☐	☐	☐
• Induction objectives	☐	☐	☐
• Annual appraisal	☐	☐	☐
• Periodic reviews	☐	☐	☐
• Personal Development Plans	☐	☐	☐
• Letters of concern	☐	☐	☐
• Personnel records	☐	☐	☐
• Aide-Memoire notes	☐	☐	☐
• Training plans	☐	☐	☐
• Objectives	☐	☐	☐
• Performance Improvement Plans	☐	☐	☐
• Disciplinary procedures	☐	☐	☐

Appendices

Appendix 4 – Aide-Memoire List

Aide-Memoire   *John Smith*

Most experienced/
knowledgeable person in
the team
01/4 -- Good quality of
work completed on a
specific project
11/6 -- Trained new team
members in H&S, good
feedback from employee
14/8 -- Sorted a problem
out no other could sort

11/4 -- Missed deadline
4/4 -- Late for work
14/4 -- Late for work
(missed bus)
14/5 -- Errors in
administration that caused
considerable disruption
11/4 -- Argued with team
members over trivial matter
14/5 -- Rude and aggressive
to new team member
23/6 -- Late in finishing
project
22/6 -- Rude and aggressive
towards customer
14/7 -- Late in finishing
project
27/8 -- Takes longer to
complete tasks than newer
employees (3 occasions)
14/9 -- Rude and aggressive
towards customer
27/9 - Argued in front of
other team members

Appendix 5 – Example Performance Improvement Plan

Performance Improvement Plan (Informal)

Name: **Fred Smith**   Position: **Customer Service Advisor**

Area for Improvement	Aim	Specific Action Required (SMART)	Start Date	Review Date
Communication with Management	Company Values taken into consideration at all times when communicating with Unit Manager	• With immediate effect, cease argumentative and hostile behaviour towards Unit Manager during discussions on performance issues. • Emotive/controversial issues must be discussed with the Unit Manager in private and not in front of other team members.	Immediate	Dec 20th
Communication with Team members	Company Values taken into consideration at all times when communicating with team members	• With immediate effect, cease hostile and argumentative behaviour towards other team members within the workplace. • Discuss controversial issues with Unit Manager **before** approaching team members.	Immediate	Dec 20th
Flexibility	Improved team/section support	Occasional 'out of normal hours' work to support section in times of high work demands.	Immediate	Dec 20th
Multi-skilling	Fully trained and proficient in one other area of the section operation	• Undertake training in Systems Support. • Attend training in modules 1 to 6 and achieve the required validation requirements. • Communicate with the Unit Manager any training concerns in the first instance.	By end July	After mod 3 completion
Performance	Carry out instructions given by Unit Manager at all times.	Carry out, to the required standard instructions given by Unit Manager. If request is viewed as 'unreasonable' it must be discussed in a rational non-emotional way.	Immediate	Dec 20th
Support & Guidance	Difficulties experienced in the achievement of this Performance Improvement Plan.	Any concerns regarding the achievement of these objectives must be communicated to Unit Manager in the first instance where additional support and guidance will be provided.	Immediate	End of PIP review period

Employee Signature *F Smith* ....   Date ... 23/9/2013 ...

Unit Manager's Signature............   Date ....   Review Date: ... 20/12/2013 ...

Appendix 6 – Example: Objective based Job Description

Line Manager Job Description

Job Purpose

To lead, motivate and develop the team in order to maximise efficiencies of the Business Unit and exceed pre-determined performance targets.

Role Expectations:

Sales and Business Development
- Achieve defined performance targets and supporting KPI's.
- Maintain costs within budgets.
- Be constantly aware of competitor marketing activities, acting accordingly to minimise loss of business to competition.
- Implement without exception all company marketing initiatives.

Service
- Fully implement company customer service procedures without exception.
- Resolve complaints effectively and commercially.

Team Performance and Development
- Provide new employees with relevant induction training.
- Monitor employee performance, setting appropriate objectives in the event of a shortfall in performance.
- Regularly review employee performance, setting appropriate development objectives where needed.
- Address consistent poor performance issues timely and procedurally.
- Identify employees with desire and potential for management, implementing appropriate PDP.

Operating Standards
- Maintain the required Health, Hygiene and Safety standards at all times.
- Ensure business unit meets the required standard of tidiness and housekeeping.
- Conduct compliance audits as per procedures, putting into place improvement actions when required.
- Report and record all Health and Safety incidents.

Communication
- Build and maintain productive working relationships with all support personnel.
- Return HO requested information speedily and to the required standard.
- Ensure employee issues and concerns are fed back when required.

Appendix 7 – Example: Poor Performance Procedures

Poor Performance Procedures

It is accepted that all employees' performance will fluctuate at times; for continued poor performance, the following procedures will be put into place by your line manager.

1. Definition of poor performance: 'When an employee's **performance** or **behaviour** falls below the required standards'.

2. Employee's rights
All employees have the following entitlements if challenged about poor performance:
- There should be evidence of poor performance
- Employees should be made aware of the exact nature of concerns
- It should be made clear to the employee the standard of performance that is expected
- Appropriate training or support should be made available to the employee for them to improve.
- The employee should be given adequate time to improve.
- It should be made clear to the employee the potential consequences of failing to achieve the required standard of performance.
- Detailed documentation should be kept at each stage of the procedure and copied to the employee.
- All employees will be treated in the same way.

3. Company Performance Management Procedures
3.1 Informal Procedures
In the event of persistent poor performance your line manager will:
- Initially sit down with you informally (one-to-one) and discuss the performance issue(s) with you and agree a way forward.
- A brief note will be made in your personal file that this conversation took place.

3.2 Semi Formal Procedures
If poor performance continues your line manager will:
- Issue you with an informal **Performance Improvement Plan** (P.I.P.) which will clearly outline what you need to achieve to reach the required standard. The Plan will also include the support you will be given and the time scales for improvement. The line manager will also inform you of the consequences of more formal discussions (disciplinary) if the required standard is not achieved as per the required timescale.
- Move to the next stage of the procedure **at any time** if insufficient effort is being made by the employee towards achieving the required standards.

Appendix 7 – Example: Poor Performance Procedures *Continued*

- Review the Performance Improvement Plan as per the set out timescales and, in the event of continued poor performance, inform you that the matter is to be discussed formally within a disciplinary interview.
- In this event the line manager will advise you of your right to be accompanied and give you sufficient time to prepare for the formal meeting.

Important note: A formal disciplinary interview does not automatically result in a formal warning. The purpose of the meeting is to discuss the situation more formally (in front of witnesses) and decide what is the appropriate action to be taken. The level of sanction (if any) will depend on the employee's reasons for their poor performance communicated at the meeting.

3.3 Formal Procedures
The line manager will conduct the formal meeting and:

- Review the Performance Improvement Plan.
- Discuss the reasons why the required level of performance is not being achieved.
- Discuss any mitigating circumstances there are as to why the standards are not being met.
- Adjourn to decide the appropriate action that is required in the circumstances.

3.1.1 Formal Warning
If the line manager issues you with a formal warning it will normally be a **1st Written Warning,** but your line manager does retain the right to issue you with a **Final Written Warning** if the situation (damage to the business or other employees) is sufficiently serious.

In the event of you being issued with a formal warning your line manager will:

- Inform you of your right to appeal and the procedures for doing so.
- Re-issue you with a **Formal Performance Improvement Plan** which again will clearly outline what you need to achieve to reach the required standard. The Plan will also include the support you will be given and time scales for improvement.
- Inform you of the consequences of even more formal discussions (2nd disciplinary interview) if the required standard is not achieved as per the required timescale.

4. Continued Poor Performance
In the event of continued poor performance, your line manager will again conduct a formal meeting and go through the same process as outlined in 3.1.1.

Important note: If an employee's performance again fails to meet the required standard, the line manager retains the right to issue the employee with a Final Written Warning or (in certain circumstances) to terminate the employee's contract with the organisation.

Appendix 8 – Example: Induction Objectives (Line Manager)

By the end of the **Induction Period** newly appointed managers will be expected to have:

Sales and Financial

- Reviewed current/historical sales and financial information, identified improvement and development opportunities, moving forward on these opportunities following discussions with line manager.

- Familiarised themselves with local competitors, identified strengths/weaknesses between the businesses and acted on information gained where appropriate.

Service

- Thoroughly reviewed Service standards, identified areas for improvement and have already implemented a number of service improvements.
- Reviewed all aspects of service planning (daily/weekly rotas, Holiday planning) to ensure that service provided meets the requirements of the customer.

Team

- Fully familiarised themselves with all team members, identified training and development requirements and have a team training plan being implemented.

- Following discussions with line manager, commenced taking appropriate action where performance or behaviour issues have been identified within the team.

Operating Standards

- Brought the Business Unit up to the required H&S and Security standards.

- Ensured that the Unit is consistently achieving the required compliance standards.

- Addressed any housekeeping issues and brought the Business Unit to a high standard of cleanliness and tidiness.

Communication

- Developed good communication between themselves, their line manager, support functions and other Unit Managers

Appendix 9 – Example: Induction Objectives (Employee)

By the end of the **Induction Period** newly appointed <u>employees</u> will be expected to be:

Sales and Financial
- Achieving the required financial targets.

Service
- Consistently working to company service procedures.
- Not causing service issues but, in the event of this happening, learning from the experience.
- Supporting the team in resolving service issues professionally and commercially.

Team
- Accepted by other team members in the business unit.
- Readily supporting other team members when required to do so.
- Actively contributing to team development and success.

Operating Standards
- Working to the required health and safety and security standards.
- Working to the required standard of tidiness and cleanliness.

Communication
- Communicating effectively with other team members and line manager.

Values -- demonstrating the following behaviours, being:
- Punctual
- Reliable
- Approachable
- Supportive of others
- Flexible
- Working to a high standard
- Honest and open
- Positive, optimistic
- Motivated

Appendix 10 – Example: Appraisal (Poor Performer)

Annual Appraisal	
• Resolving IT issues • Administration organisation • Punctuality • Working under pressure	• Handling service issues • Working within the team • Supporting team during times of high workload • Attendance • Meeting deadlines • Communicating with line manager

Manager Comments:

Fred is very competent when working on his own and produces good quality work but 'working within the team' and 'consistency of performance' have been my main concerns this year (hence the formal discussion that took place in July). Fred needs to realise that there is nothing personal here; we are only trying to get him to perform and behave to the required standard: the objectives outlined in the PIP he is currently working on will certainly give him the direction needed. I have every confidence in Fred achieving the required standard and will continue to provide him with the support needed to get him there.

Objectives for the following Year:
- Meet the required standard as outlined in the Performance Improvement Plan
- Team working – More support required within team during times of high workload
- Handling challenging service issues
- Attendance

Employees' comments:
I do not entirely agree with my performance assessment as I feel more consideration should have been made to my many positive aspects rather than my negative ones. I will work towards achieving my objectives but I will need more training in some areas.

Appendix 11 – Example: Company Values

These are real values as set by the Founder and Chairman of a major UK Furniture Business:

Integrity; Doing the right things when nobody is watching

Sense of Urgency; Do it now attitude, touch it once, decisive with priorities, purposeful, determined

Hard Working; In early, last out, industrious, keeps at it consistently, sticks to it until the job is done

Enthusiasm; Passionate about the job/company, genuine smile/positive nature, keen and eager to do things

Takes Responsibility; Accepts ownership of issues, does not blame others, does not walk by issues

Respectful Communication; Respectful of all colleagues, not arrogant, egotistical or superior with others

Getting stuck in; Jacket off, muck in when required to do so, prepared to get hands dirty when necessary

Down to Earth; Normal and unpretentious, practical in the way they work, realistic and sensible

Achieving Measures Set; Focuses on achieving targets and objectives

Handling adversity; Bounces back from adversity, structured when required to bring sales back on track

Keep it Simple; Does not over-complicate issues, keeps commercial reality in perspective

Common Sense; Demonstrates a realistic, sensible approach when dealing with commercial issues

Customer Focused; Sees and understands the commercial aspects of poor service

Maintain High Standards; Behaves appropriately in different situations

Fair and Reasonable; Acts fairly, reasonably and objectively when dealing with interpersonal issues

Consistent; Know where you stand, no up or down in style, not a moody person, always positive, enthusiastic

Confidentiality; Keeps business and 'people confidential' information to oneself

Positive Atmosphere; Optimistic attitude even in times of adversity or setback

Self-development and learning; Open to reviewing self, identifying development requirements and taking personal action to learn and develop

Loyalty; Faithfully working to commitments or obligations.

Appendix 12 – Personal Improvement Plan

Private and Confidential
Personal Improvement Plan

To:	Fred Smith
From:	A. Manager
Ref:	Personal Improvement Plan

Fred,

The aim of this **Improvement Plan** is to bring your behaviour to the required standard. As discussed at our meeting on the 14th June, my main areas of concern are: disruption at team meetings, disrespectful behaviour towards the younger, more junior, team members and your argumentative behaviour towards myself in front of other team members. If you do not adhere to the actions outlined in the plan, I will have no choice other than to move the matter to a more formal stage.

Communication at team briefings
- Cease negative, derisory comments to other team members during team briefings. If there are any negative comments to be made, discuss with line manager (in private) after meeting.

Behaviour towards other team members
- Cease negative, derisory comments to other team members during team briefings. If there are any negative comments to be made, discuss them with me (in private) after meeting.
- Be less impatient and disrespectful towards new team members.

Communication with Line Manager
- Listen to managers' comments and feedback before making assumptions and becoming argumentative and emotional
- Hold back on negative comments to line manager until in private.

Appendix 13 – Example: Letter of Concern

Private and Confidential
Letter of Concern

To: Fred Smith
From: A. Manager
Ref: Inconsistency of Performance

Fred,

I am issuing this **letter of concern** because of your inconsistency of work performance, as I have had to speak to you on numerous occasions regarding the accuracy and timeliness of your administration.

As I mentioned on our meeting on the 26th June, this inconsistency is resulting in much disruption within the department and causing me to allocate additional resources to check the quality of your work.

Although I am not seeing this issue as a formal matter at this stage, I need to communicate to you the consequences of formal action if I do not see an immediate improvement in the accuracy and timeliness in your administration.

You have in the past shown that you can achieve the required standard, so I do not believe this to be a competence issue but a personal motivation matter.

Please perform to the required standard.

Appendix 14 – Example Sickness Record

Sickness and Absence Record

Surname: *Smith*

Forenames: *John*

Payroll no. *1418*

DOS: *August 1997*

DOB: *11th October 1973*

Sickness Entitlement: *20 Days Entitlement*

Month	Total
April	2
May	1
June	6
July	1
August	2
September	1
October	1
November	1
December	2
January	1
February	2
March	
	20

Key

SP: Sickness Paid
SU: Sickness Unpaid

Appendix 15 – Bradford Factor Explained

The Bradford Factor

Short, frequent and unplanned absences are more disruptive than longer absences. A one-off long period of absence can be managed, where as numerous short-term periods are unmanageable, disruptive and costly. The Bradford factor is a simple calculation that can be used to highlight frequent, short-term employee sick leave.

The Bradford Factor is calculated as follows:

$$S^2 \times D = B$$

- S is the total number of spells (instances) of absence of an individual over a set period

- D is the total number of days of absence of that individual over the same set period

- B is the Bradford Factor score

Using this formula, frequent short absences will quickly rack up a higher Bradford Factor score than less frequent absences:

Example:
Six days of absence in a period of a year will give different scores, depending on the number of absences.

- One spell of six days sickness would equate to 1(S) x 1(S) x 6(D) = 6 points
- Two spells of sickness would equate to 2(S) x 2(S) x 6(D) = 24 points
- Three spells of sick leave would equate to 3(S) x 3(S) x 6(D) = 54 points

All these cases involve a total of six days total absence, but where there were three occasions of sick leave, the score is considerably higher; cases of this nature may prompt formal managerial action quicker then otherwise.

Appendix 16 – Example: Self Certification Form

SELF CERTIFICATE OF ABSENCE

If absence exceeds seven calendar days a doctor's certificate is required.

Name _____ *John Smith* _____

Position _____ *Sales Associate* _____

First day of sickness _____ *Saturday 13th August 2011* _____

Last day of sickness _____ *Saturday 13th August 2011* _____

Number of working days sick _____ *1* _____

Date of return to work _____ *Monday 15th August 2011* _____

Absence was due to the following reason

_____ *Stomach problems* _____

_____

_____

EMPLOYEE DECLARATION

I have ⟨have not⟩ consulted a doctor.
I have ⟨have not⟩ filled in and sent off a Sickness Benefits Form.

I declare to the best of my knowledge the above information is true.

Signed: _____ *John Smith* _____ Date: _____ *15/8/2011* _____

Countersigned _____ *A. Manager* _____ Date: _____ *15/8/2011* _____

Notification received from: _____

Date: _____ Time: _____

Appendix 17 – Example: Issues and Actions List

Issues and Actions List

Issue – Deadlines and Documentation Accuracy

Actions:
- Contact supervisor before deadline time if there is a concern about a timescale
- Re-training on all documentation completion procedures by end of month
- Double check all information before submitting

Issue – Negative response to feedback on performance

Actions:
- Manager to give warning of feedback meeting to give time to prepare
- Review each feedback session on completion to ensure clarity of actions and effectiveness of discussion

Issue – Time-Keeping and Attendance

Actions:
- On all occassions contact office if going to be late
- When late, report to manager on arrival
- Attend 'Return to Work' interview on all instances of absence

Appendix 18 – Example: Note on File

Private and Confidential

Personal Record

Name: _____ Position: _____ Start Date:

_____

24/4   Pay rise 2%

26/4   Attended company administration course

04/5   Annual review

18/5   Managed department during manager's absence

24/6   Good report completed for department strategy

02/7   Complaint received from employee regarding

       aggressive behaviour

11/7   Informally warned for aggressive behaviour towards

       new team members

20/7   Sent home from work because of drinking spree

       during lunch break, unfit to face customers

28/7   Mid-year review conducted, spoken to about both

       behaviour and attendance

Appendix 19 – Bullying and Harassment Behaviour Summary

Bullying Actions and Behaviours:
- Yelling and screaming
- Using inappropriate language i.e. Swearing
- Angry outbursts directed at them
- Aggressive posture, invading their personal space
- Using aggressive hand gestures
- Undermining them behind their back
- Ridiculing - making them look stupid
- Name calling
- Inappropriate comments on personal appearance
- Malicious teasing
- Playing pranks and practical jokes
- Negative comments in front of others

Harassment Actions and Behaviours:
- Offensive remarks
- Innuendos, Unfair comments
- Unnecessary one-on-one contact
- Subjective words
- Personal contact
- Invading someone's personal space

Abuse of Power:
- Giving excessive and harsh criticism of work performance
- Isolating employees from each other by delegating tasks aimed at keeping them apart
- Ignoring the employee
- Holding back productive work
- Distributing workload unfairly
- Requesting unnecessary work to be done
- Setting unachievable deadlines
- Setting unachievable task and objectives
- Undermining work performance
- Devaluing work effort
- Failing to give credit where credit is due

Appendix 20 – Your Personal Development Plan

Poor performance management is the most challenging of all the management duties because no other task requires so much **knowledge**, the use of so many **skills** and the need for so many personal **qualities**. Assess your knowledge, skill and personal qualities here, highlight four of your most important development areas and formulate your PDP.

Priority

Knowledge:
- Legislation on Disciplinary and Dismissal procedures ☐
- ACAS procedures ☐
- Company Culture ☐
- Company disciplinary procedures ☐
- Company procedures relating to HR Management ☐
- Job roles and responsibilities ☐

Skills:
- Note taking skills ☐
- Report/memo writing Skills ☐
- Giving feedback ☐
- Assertiveness skills ☐
- Reviewing skills ☐
- Appraisal skills ☐
- Presenting and explaining skills ☐
- Selling and persuasion skills ☐
- Influencing skills ☐
- Listening Skills ☐

Personal Qualities
- Courage ☐
- Confidence ☐
- Persistence ☐
- Patience ☐
- Determination ☐
- Honesty ☐

Appendix 20 – Your Personal Development Plan Continued

Personal Development Plan

Personal Development Objective:
'To be confident and skilled in poor performance management'

Development Area:	
Action Plan:	*By When*

Development Area:	
Action Plan:	*By When*

Development Area:	
Action Plan:	*By When*

Development Area:	
Action Plan:	*By When*

Notes and Learning

Notes and Learning